Wholeness and Holiness

How to Be Sane, Spiritual, and Saintly

DAVID RICHO

ORBIS BOOKS
Maryknoll, New York 10545

Founded in 1970, Orbis Books endeavors to publish works that enlighten the mind, nourish the spirit, and challenge the conscience. The publishing arm of the Maryknoll Fathers and Brothers, Orbis seeks to explore the global dimensions of the Christian faith and mission, to invite dialogue with diverse cultures and religious traditions, and to serve the cause of reconciliation and peace. The books published reflect the views of their authors and do not represent the official position of the Maryknoll Society. To learn more about Orbis Books, please visit our website at www.orbisbooks.com.

Library of Congress Cataloging-in-Publication Data

Names: Richo, David, 1940– author.
Title: Wholeness and holiness : how to be sane, spiritual, and saintly / David Richo.
Description: Maryknoll, New York : Orbis Books, 2020. | Includes bibliographical references. | Summary: "Wholeness and Holiness guides us through a three-step journey to psychological soundness, spiritual wholeness, and saintly holiness. To attain this goal, a person must work at all three"— Provided by publisher.
Identifiers: LCCN 2019039423 (print) | LCCN 2019039424 (ebook) | ISBN 9781626983533 (paperback) | ISBN 9781608338184 (ebook)
Subjects: LCSH: Psychology, Religious. | Christianity—Psychology. | Psychology—Religious aspects. | Spiritual formation. | Holiness—Christianity.
Classification: LCC BR110 .R53 2020 (print) | LCC BR110 (ebook) | DDC 248.4—dc23
LC record available at https://lccn.loc.gov/2019039423
LC ebook record available at https://lccn.loc.gov/2019039424

To all my grandchildren

And in tender memory of my dear Aunt Tess
and of my friend and guide Barbara Marx Hubbard

No thing that ever flew,
Not the lark, not you,
Can die as others do.
—EDNA ST. VINCENT MILLAY

Contents

Introduction

*An inner wholeness keeps pressing its still unfulfilled
claims upon us.*

—EMMA JUNG, *THE GRAIL LEGEND*

Our lifetime on this earth offers us three magnificent chances to
evolve into the fullness of our humanity:

> We can become wholly who we are.
> We can be wholesome in how we act.
> We can be holy in how we live.

The first requires psychological work and reflection. The second
calls for spiritual awareness and practices. The third is a grace that
leads to dedicated action.

From a psychological perspective, sanity is needed to survive and
thrive in the world. The development of our body-mind is fulfilled
when we are psychologically sound. In this book, sanity is not simply the opposite of madness. It is defined as full mental health and
exuberant well-being.

From a wholeness perspective, we feel a longing in ourselves
for something more than individual surviving and thriving. We are
oriented toward an ever-expanding spiritual consciousness. The
evolution of our body-mind is fulfilled when we are spiritually
motivated.

From a faith perspective, we believe that sanctity is our divinely imprinted calling and destiny. The divine purpose of our body-mind is fulfilled when we are saintly in our choices.

These three intertwine and beam out to the world as three rays of one sun, fully actualized personhood.

The self-help movement sometimes gives the impression that its recommendations are separate from spiritual practices. Spiritually oriented books might propose the reverse. In this book we look for ways to bring the two together: psychological health and spiritual consciousness. But we won't stop there. Our work-practice escorts us to a third splendid possibility: becoming a saint, which is attainable by everyone and everyone's highest life fulfillment.

The meaning and purpose of sanity, spirituality, and sanctity keep evolving. The definition of an elbow has remained the same throughout the centuries because it is what it is, no matter what is happening socially or politically. But the definitions of sanity, spirituality, and sanctity change over time since they are directly influenced by what is happening in the world. All three, unlike an elbow, are *interactive*, directly influenced by contemporary issues and necessarily responsive to society's needs. In the twenty-first century, our world is more tightly interconnected than ever. Environmental concerns, societal issues, and the political scene are crucial to the design and maintenance of our mental health, our spirituality, and the shape of our saintly calling. Thus, social consciousness and social action are important themes throughout this book as we describe what it takes today to be sane, spiritual, and saintly.

The good news is that sanity, spirituality, and sanctity have a playbook. Each of the three has a specific set of practices that actualize them. We will explore these practices individually and discover how to weave them into our daily life, work, feelings, and sense of who we really are and why we are here.

We see psychological *sanity* as a *foundation* and *spirituality* as a *bridge*. They are not the complete story of wholeness. Sanity is a beginning.

Spirituality is a conduit. Neither one nor both constitute the completion of a life of wholeness. Neither can go far enough as we come to see sanctity as our ultimate goal. Sanctity is our full aliveness, personal fulfillment, the divine completion of a human life, the presence of holiness on earth. Our challenge is to integrate not two but three resplendent trails to humanness.

All three options remain choices that are being offered to us. Some people choose to go no further than psychological health. Some people deny that there is a spiritual or saintly dimension at all, while others may focus on spiritual practices and neglect mental health concerns. Some people focus on both. We can do what psychology recommends and become truly healthy. We can engage in spiritual practices and grow in transcendent ways. But we can also combine union with the divine, heroic giving, dedicated focus, and full openness to grace—and thereby journey toward sanctity.

Sanctity is not limited to famous people like Joan of Arc or Archbishop Oscar Romero. The single mother who cares so single-mindedly for her children is certainly a saintly heroine. Saintly heroism refers to selfless love, dedicated service, bold courage, heart-centered focus, and willingness to risk one's safety and security. It includes a turning from ego-centeredness to social consciousness, universal love, and unlimited caring. We need not be daunted by the bigness of this enterprise. We can firmly trust that we do not hear a call without being given sufficient graces for fulfilling it. This is how sanctity is a synchronous blend of abundant love that we keep showing and boundless grace that we keep receiving. Grace is the gift dimension of life, available in all three stages of our growth.

Spirituality and holiness both flourish optimally in an atmosphere of psychological health. Likewise, wholeness happens best in the context of a life of goodness with a commitment to co-create a world of justice, peace, and love—our spiritual goals. Holiness happens in those special times when we soar beyond psychological health and spiritual wholesomeness. We are given the grace to go over the top in our virtue, over and above what is required, above and beyond what is expected, past spiritual practices, beyond the call of duty. We embrace the unrequired extra that makes us saints: we love in daring ways; we access wisdom beyond ordinary knowledge; we usher healing, even miracles, into our world. From the Christian perspective, such a world is the kingdom of God, the completion of all things in Christ.

Every human person, with or without religion, can walk through this sacred door since sanctity can happen in myriad ways. We can be big saints or little saints: We can say yes to moments of saintliness, internally or externally, and that may be enough. We can say yes to a lifetime of sanctity, and that will be more than enough. Each person is called to sanctity, but the spectrum is wide—as wide as human nature itself. One saintly act is all it takes for success.

None of the three goals is expected to be fulfilled all the time. No one is sane, spiritual, and saintly every minute of the day. Our daily expectations of ourselves are appropriate when they are "good enough":

> We are sane almost all the time.
> We are spiritual most of the time.
> We are saintly from time to time.

Let's consider the origin of some of these words. "Sanity" is from the Latin *sanus*, which means health, soundness of body and mind. "Spirituality" is from the Latin *spiritalis* for "breathing," since an empowering Spirit breathes through us, lives in us, acts through us. "Sanctity" is from the Latin *sanctus*, meaning holy or sacred. For Christians, saints manifest the sacred indwelling presence of the Holy Spirit, the divine energy of wisdom and love, the *experience* of the sacred. "Wholeness" and "holiness" derive from German and Dutch words with similar meanings: unimpaired, thorough, full, and integral.

All three levels of our development—sanity, spirituality, and sanctity—work in concert. Throughout this book we focus on the three elements and show how to bring them together. No one of them interferes with any other.

Let's use the example of healthy assertiveness to see how the three goals interflow. Our psychological work shows us how to ask for what we want, express our needs, and protect our boundaries. When we bring a spiritual consciousness to those goals we also ask for societal justice, speak up about injustice, and take a stand to protect others as equal in value to ourselves. In saintliness, we put ourselves on the line as we do this. We extend our caring compassion without stint or limit. We put ourselves second, if to do so will be vital to someone else's survival. We speak truth to power even when it may land us in big trouble.

Sanity, spirituality, and sanctity all include both consciousness and practice, awareness and action:

- When we are *psychologically healthy*, we are aware of ourselves, our feelings, our talents, our limitations. We then make wise choices that help us fulfill our personal goals and contribute to the world around us. It is up to us to nurture this process. When we do, we feel wholesome—body, heart, and mind. Sanity is goal-oriented. A goal is a purpose we strive to fulfill so that our lives can be satisfactory.

- When we are *spiritually vibrant* we are aware of the transcendent radiance in the universe and engage in actions that promote its conscious evolution. Spirituality is dedicated to a unique destiny, something more than a goal. It is the fulfillment of our life purpose. In this book, the word "destiny" does not mean predetermined or fated. It refers to the unfolding of our full capacity for humanness.

- When we are *saintly* we are aware of the presence of God in all things and in every moment. We then take every opportunity to act in accord with the divine resolve to co-create an evolved world. We are thoroughly convinced that everything is holy. In this book, we use the word "God" in a nondual way. God is the wholeness-holiness in us and in all things.

One does not have to be a traditional believer or member of a church to be a saint. We might, for instance, still be on board for sanctity when we say, "I don't know if there is a God but I want to act as if there were a God and as if this God were love."

Each of the three goals of a fully human life—sanity, spirituality, and sanctity—places a uniquely thrilling spin on our sense of ourselves:

- When we are sound in body and mind, our sense of ourselves is unreserved self-esteem. We are self-confident and secure. We can step up to the plate when curveballs are pitched our way. We maintain equanimity in the midst of chaos. We still appreciate and seek validation from others but now we self-validate more often.

- When we are spiritually oriented, our sense of ourselves is expanded consciousness. Pierre Teilhard de Chardin, in *The Human Phenomenon*, describes it best when he states that we have "ever more perfect eyes at the heart of a cosmos where it is always possible to discern more."[1] Our sense of self spiritually is also responsiveness to our unique calling to make the world more just and peaceful than it is now—to make ourselves more loving than we have been yet.

- As saints, our sense of ourselves is total gratitude for the graces we receive and total willingness to embrace the heroic challenges the world keeps tossing in our direction. This includes a sense of ordination to a holy calling: "You are a chosen race, a royal priesthood, a holy nation, God's own people, in order that you

---

[1] Pierre Teilhard de Chardin, *The Human Phenomenon: A New Edition and Translation of* Le phenemene humain, trans. Sarah Appleton-Weber (East Sussex, UK: Sussex Academic Press, 2003), 3.

may proclaim the mighty acts of him who called you out of darkness into his marvelous light" (1 Pet 2:9).

Thus, our progress in any of the three S's does not rely only on our actions. Something in us is contributing to making full humanness happen. Carl Jung, in "Concerning Mandala Symbolism," states it clearly: "There is in the psyche a process that seeks its own goal no matter what the external factors may be . . . the almost irresistible compulsion and urge to become what one is."[2]

Aristotle used the word "entelechy" to refer to this inner life force in every being to grow up into what it really is. An instinctive energy within us directs the growth of our body-minds to actualize the full breadth of our identity. We aren't becoming herons; we are becoming full-on humans. We are becoming by natural predisposition what we have the capacity to be. Our human entelechy is an ineradicable, irrepressible arc in the direction of all the rainbow colors of self-emergence: sanity, spirituality, and sanctity.

This stunning power is the foundation of our trust in our bodies, minds, emotions, and spirit. Something alive inside is infallibly oriented to full self-emergence. We align ourselves with the entelechy of sanity when we make healthy choices. We align spiritually when we go beyond our apparent limits into the transcendent. We align in holiness when we live in harmony with the voice and movements of the indwelling Spirit.

When we see someone in trouble and have only psychology to help us make sense of it we might say, "That's happening over there, and I am over here." This may be safety-making, but it is also separation-making. This is a minimum opening of our entelechy. In spiritual awareness and commitment we ask what the Good Samaritan might ask: "How am I part of this suffering, and how can I be a force of healing?" In saintliness, we see someone suffering and we do not say,

---

[2] Carl G. Jung, "Concerning Mandala Symbolism," in *Mandala Symbolism* (Princeton, NJ: Princeton University Press, 1962), 73.

"There but for the grace of God go I." We say, "There by the grace of God go I." Our compassion flows from irresistible communion—the ultimate and full expression of our human entelechy as a deep *kinship*. Father Greg Boyle, SJ, wrote about kinship as "not serving the other, but being one with the other. . . . Jesus was not 'a man for others'; he was one with them. There is a world of difference in that."[3]

In this book we take a three-step journey, however gingerly, to psychological soundness, spiritual wholeness, and saintly holiness. They form the mystical rose of three petals all unfolded, the gift of wholeness and holiness at the end and all throughout our human journey.

In any here and now, we can check in with ourselves about our three spectacular human enterprises. As a daily practice, we can also ask ourselves three questions. The first is about sanity, the second about spirituality, the third about sanctity:

- What opportunity do I have today to be healthy, both physically and psychologically? What opportunity do I have to be healthy, both physically and psychologically, in this very moment?
- What spiritual destiny can I give myself to today? What is the door, the on-ramp I see before me in this moment?
- What graces of wisdom and daring action can I take advantage of today? What love in my heart is opening now so that I can be a channel of grace?

We ask for this reliable grace now as we embark upon our marvel-filled pilgrimage to no fewer than three shrines: sanity, spirituality, and sanctity. They will appear together as the one destination of the Camino of this lifetime. Indeed, they show us why we have been given a lifetime.

---

[3] Greg Boyle, SJ, *Tattoos on the Heart: The Power of Boundless Compassion* (New York: Free Press, 2010), 72.

PART ONE

SANITY

1

What Is Sanity?

A deeper, broader sense of the self, which is already whole, already content, already filled with abundant life . . .

—RICHARD ROHR, *JUST THIS*

Sanity—mental health—is a state of flow and well-being; being grounded, resilient, and balanced; possessing self-esteem; and being able to adjust to the events of life. We experience such mental health in many ways. Here are the main examples:

- We do what it takes to fulfill our physical and psychological goals of surviving and thriving.
- We have a sense of self-worth.
- We generally have peace of mind and openness of heart.
- We trust our abilities and our inner resources.
- We are capable of coping with the stresses of daily life resiliently.
- We are able to flow with our ever-changing circumstances, feelings, and moods.
- We align ourselves with reality rather than illusion.
- We make peace with our past.
- We recognize our triggers and do not fall prey to inappropriate reactions to them.
- We see through and deal with our own self-generated anxieties.
- Our fears do not stop or drive us.

- We are able to work effectively both alone and with others.
- We are able to balance work and play.
- We can put off immediate gratification in favor of long-term goals.
- We are assertive enough to ask for what we want, express our feelings, and stand up for what we believe.
- We live in accord with our own deepest needs, values, and wishes rather than those of others.
- We are free of inhibition, hiding, or escaping, especially through addictions.
- We are able to respect others' boundaries and preserve our own while remaining flexible.
- We have the capacity to trust others when appropriate.
- We are trustworthy in our relationships.
- We are able to build an intimate relationship and be effective in it, if this fits our life goal and personality. We realize, without judgment, that not everyone is suited for an intimate relationship.
- We can work on conflicts that may arise in ourselves and our relationships, or we seek professional help.
- We can monitor our ego so that we act respectfully and cooperatively with others.
- We contribute to our community.
- We accept the things we cannot change; we take steps to change what needs to be changed; we keep gaining the wisdom to know the difference.
- We have a sense of humor and optimism most of the time.

Together, these constitute the main ingredients of a healthy personality. We find them in any Psychology 101 textbook. We do notice, however, that they may be interpreted within an Anglo-Saxon cultural bias of rugged individualism. A full description of a healthy personality cannot be based entirely on the recommendations of Freud and other northern European physicians. They were, at times, caught in Cartesian dualisms, dividing mind and body, conscious and unconscious, individual and social. An integrated view is unlikely to emerge from those divisions. In this book we keep in mind that mental health only happens fully in a context of support from and collaboration with others. Otherwise, it is not in keeping with our social nature. We are not "the little engine that could." We are part of a fleet, every vessel helping all the others, only arriving at our port of call together.

Our individual goals certainly reflect our lifestyle and history. But we also have common goals such as co-creating communities of co-operation, co-forming a world of interdependence, and co-caring for our planet. *As we change the lens through which we look out at the world, we begin to look out for the world.* The combination of sanity, spirituality, and sanctity forms a unified foundation for that achievement. Indeed, we progress as individuals only as the evolution of all beings progresses. This takes conscious connection and collaboration, propellers of evolution.

A theme throughout this book is that there is no such thing as psychological-only, spiritual-only, or saintly-only. Our mental health matters to us from a psychological point of view. With spiritual awareness, everyone's wholeness matters. With holy caring, we give anything to help it happen for the world. All three of these form one living arc.

We remind ourselves that no one is totally consistent in health habits, mental or otherwise. As we saw above, our goal is good enough, not flawless, mental health. This means that we feel basically good about ourselves, have a generally happy life, and have reasonably successful relationships. We seek not perfection, a chimera, only an ever-blossoming commitment to stay on the healthy path as best we can. An algebraic term, "asymptote," offers an analogy. It is a curve that keeps approaching a line on a graph *but never reaches it.* That describes our path; we keep approaching while never fully arriving—and that is acceptable to us. Our intention endures purely, perfectly. Our actions may not always follow suit. When they don't, we look for ways to repair ourselves and we get back on track. When they do, we like ourselves more, a sign of self-esteem.

2

Discovering Who We Are

Our body-heart-minds are playgrounds of thought, intuition, imagination, feeling, sensation, need, longing, mood, words, and actions. Each and all of these reveal the *real* us to ourselves. Our healthy criteria for what we choose to be, say, and do are, "Does this reflect my true self? Does this contract or expand my whole self?" To become what you really are is the first divine summons to each of us.

We can learn about who we are, personality-wise, by our honest replies to questions such as these:

> What are my most frequent fantasies?
> What are my ongoing desires?
> What is my consistent behavior?

Our fantasies tell us what excites us. Our desires and longings show us what we believe will fulfill us. What we do shows us what we are up to in the world—what we really want.

In neuroscience terminology, doing what feels good, what gives us pleasure, produces *dopamine*. This hormone, unfortunately, can arouse craving. We want more and more, never finding satisfaction. Our behavior can turn into a habit and then into an addiction. An alternative is happiness, the state of mind that occurs through the release of *serotonin*. Now we are pleased to feel we have enough. We know ourselves more deeply by which of the two styles appears more frequently in our lives.

The thinking mind is low on the totem pole of choice-making. We all notice that in the supermarket our desire for dopamine overrides healthy choices and we go for the cookies rather than the cauliflower. We don't always act from a motivation of pleasure or happiness. Sometimes we do what brings us pain. We might keep repeating a self-destructive behavior. We might stay too long in a dead-end job or relationship. We might still believe that we are here on earth to endure suffering rather than to be happy.

Do we keep doing what doesn't work? Do we stay stuck or do we look for help so that a change can happen? This choice also tells us who we are. Being stuck is opposed to the inner orientation of moving forward on a journey—the evolutionary drive in all of us. But whatever has become unhealthy in us is not the final word. We always have inner resources and we can always engage in practices that move us toward psychological health. Sometimes "stuckness" is connected to trauma. If that is the case, we can find help from a therapist trained in trauma/somatic work. We then progress, albeit slowly and patiently. Even the slowest pace is still a journey.

Our Concerns

In Buddhism we learn of "Eight Worldly Concerns." These givens of life also give us clues to who we are. They are sets of opposites: joy and pain, fame and obscurity, praise and blame, gain and loss. All of these happen to everyone. We might hold four of them as hopes, showing what we go for; four can be fears, showing what we try to avoid. We know ourselves when we see clearly what we are looking for and what we are running from:

> We hope for happiness and fear suffering.
> We hope for fame and fear unimportance or
> oblivion.

We hope for praise and fear blame.

We hope for gain and fear loss.

St. Paul has a similar list of comparisons: "In honor and dishonor, in ill repute and good repute. We are treated as impostors, and yet are true; as unknown, and yet are well known" (2 Cor 6:8–9). By examining our hopes and fears about each of the concerns, we understand ourselves and so many of our choices. Our hopes show us our inclinations; our fears show us our inhibitions.

Storybook Characters

Characters in stories to which we keep returning tell us about archetypal qualities in the human collective. Each represents an energy in us that may not yet be fully visible in our daily life. What is important is to see how all the characters in the stories represent features of ourselves. For instance, we are like Luke Skywalker, but at times we are also like Darth Vader; we are like Dorothy, but also like the wicked witch. We all have a light and dark side. To use an analogy, we might say that we go through life with a watchdog on one side of us and a wolf on the other. We sometimes feed one, sometimes the other. We all feed both in the course of life, no matter how saintly or errant we are. Thus, Mother St. Teresa's wolf did not starve and neither did Hitler's dog.

From a spiritual and saintly perspective, our identity is something like the faith view of the Eucharist. Under the appearance of who we are in the world is our true divinity/identity. Then we too are a holy sacrament, outward signs of inward grace that can nourish the world. Likewise, all the cosmos is sacramental. We can come to see all that is, both ourselves and all natural things, beaming from the monstrance of the universe. We come to see all that is as a bodily holding of a divine presence. When this happens in us, we are truly engaging in perpetual adoration. Our wholeness has become holiness.

3

Going from Empty to Full

Wholeness is a universal human quality though it does not always show itself in our thoughts and actions. We might have doubted ourselves and made choices that abridged the full version of ourselves. We might doubt our bigness, preferring to shear our oaken size to bonsai. But wholeness is always present within us, and accessible immediately.

We might trust the fact of our wholeness once we realize that it does not refer to perfection but to all-ness. Wholeness, psychologically, simply means that we are fully, all ourselves. We have *all* it takes to accommodate *all* that happens to us and around us. Wholeness, spiritually, means that we can rely on an inner spiritual director, always on tap, always wise, always alive in us and enlivening us. Wholeness, sanctity-wise, is grace that takes us beyond our minds to divine wisdom, beyond our immediate circle of friends to universal caring, beyond individuality to full connection with all humanity. This grace is always available in and around us.

In contemporary psychological understanding, there is no stable self but ever-shifting versions of self in accord with the people or circumstances with whom we interact. Ultimately, the conventional self is like a film—a series of discrete images that look like one continuous flow but are actually multiple and discontinuous. We are a collection of petals around no core. We are bees around no narcissus. Our personality characteristics are identifying marks, identifiable traits, but not our final identity. We are more than what we look like or act like, yet our visible, conventional, individual self is simultaneously real as a necessary convenience so that we can get through our days effectively. To believe in a stable identity makes life simple and straightforward. Our belief helps us navigate through the busy world and maintain boundaries in it. A "self" is how we organize our sense of reality and our sense of personal identity.

In Buddhism, there is no solid self behind our ordinary individuality. Instead, our identity consists of an interrelatedness with all beings, empty of separate, independent existence. "Empty" in this context means not having a stand-alone reality. Indeed, there is nothing in the entire universe hanging around anywhere on its own, apart from everything else. As humans, we are built like everything in nature's ecology: each one of us is unique, yet each is connected, linked in the interlaced web of life. Using a metaphor, we can say that a lilac is a lilac not a bee, but its existence is tied inextricably to visits from the hive. In that sense, neither the lilac nor the bee has a truly separate identity. Each is empty of separate existence; each is intimately related to the other and to all beings. As John Muir writes, "When we try to pick out anything by itself [in nature], we find it is hitched to everything else in the universe."[1]

Ironically, if there were a separate self it would not be a resource. A lone scarecrow does not offer anything to hold onto. The interrelated self is a true resource since, by it, we are participants in the whole pageant of being.

In Western psychology, we have a habitual tendency to think of our individual self as a solidity. Yet when we become absorbed in gazing at our identity as separate, we are lost. Like the vain Narcissus, we are soon destroyed by a misplaced fealty to the illusions of separateness and personal permanence. Narcissus was not as smart as the flower narcissus that accepts and loves its impermanent but glorious place in the ongoing procession of nature.

---

[1] John Muir, *My First Summer in the Sierra* (Boston: Mariner Books, 2011), 83.

Yet, in moments of enlightenment, we are whisked away from the seductive image in the glassy lake; we peep instead into our brilliant larger life, our higher self, Buddha nature, or Christ consciousness. We then see so much more than what we thought or dared to imagine. Nothing can succeed in luring us to cling to it, so we don't have to hold on anymore. Nothing is scaring us, so we don't have to run anywhere. Nothing is damming our river cruise, so our boat is in full sail.

How does all this connect to building the inner resources that make for sanity? The more we can tolerate multiple versions of ourselves and let go of the belief that there is a central, stable, nonconnected self, the more open we become. Ordinarily, we walk around with a head full of ideas, beliefs, needs, and wishes, and a body full of conditionings and habits. All that seems to constitute a self. Yet it is only the surface, like the surface of the ocean. Just below it is a vast world of pure openness (a better word to describe our inner life than void or emptiness). That open space is ever actualizing itself through our personal story. We can call it a higher self than our ego-personality. No matter the name, within us is an unlimited, undefined, unnamed potential for utter openness. We open into it through sanity, spirituality, and sanctity.

The table on the following page provides a helpful summary of the comparisons between the ego in psychology and the higher Self in spirituality and sanctity.

Regarding the integration of sanity, spirituality, and sanctity, let us consider an analogy, the metamorphosis of a caterpillar. It transcends the fuzzy but in the moment true version of itself. It is then transformed into the glory of its own full identity—what was there all the time just waiting to appear. With practice, we too transcend sanity alone to become the spiritually alive saints who we always and already are. All we leave behind is the part of us that was afraid of this extraordinary transfiguration.

Ego self (small "s")	Higher Self
Our here-and-now body-mind	A larger, deeper life force within and around us
Personal	Transpersonal
Unique to each of us	The same in everyone
Believed to be a separate freestanding identity	Linked to all beings, interdependent in the web of life, one with nature
Conditioned by our genes and history	Unconditioned and unlimited
A combination of personality traits	Universal archetypes in all of us
Body-encapsulated	Embodied and beyond the body
Alive in us from birth to death	Unborn, undying, with no beginning or end
Time-bound	Timeless
Continually changing	Unchanging
Can be incomplete	Ever-complete and whole
On a journey	Always and already arrived
Operates on an individualized level of knowledge	Holds the wisdom of the ages
Mostly comprehensible	Mostly mysterious
Has one astrological sign	Contains the entire zodiac
Our conventional identity	Equivalent of a higher power in and beyond us

4

How Childhood and Its Wounds Help Us to Know Ourselves

The journey with father and mother up and down many ladders represents the making conscious of infantile contents that have not yet been integrated. . . . This personal unconscious must always be dealt with first. . . . Otherwise the gateway to the cosmic unconscious cannot be opened.

—CARL G. JUNG, *PSYCHOLOGY AND ALCHEMY*

In an ideal psychological atmosphere, our parents and others are models of sane, healthy behavior. Spiritually, they help us form appropriate values and act with integrity. They imbue us with a sense of neighborliness toward others. They foster a beneficent worldview. We come to see ourselves as important participants in the vast evolutionary project of stewardship for this so often imperiled earth. We then feel called to be blissful saints. Thus, psychological development, a spiritual journey, and a saintly manner can happen in us simultaneously.

When we focus on our psychological development, we realize the impact of our parenting, both positive and negative. Some of us have come from healthy childhoods. Some of us have come from wounded childhoods, in which we were not nurtured or in which we were neglected or abused.

Yet, with an integrated view of sanity, spirituality, and sanctity, we do not overlook the presence of a higher power in our lives that is fatherly and motherly, brotherly and sisterly. We feel cared for, guided, and supported in our holy desire to be familial toward others. In everything we seek and find for ourselves, we look for ways to offer it to others. Our spiritual and saintly orientation adds that dimension.

As we grow in our threefold way, we move from the story of "a wound inflicted on me by them." We grieve our hurts without needing to retaliate. We appreciate how our wounds help us open to our full self: *Through my own tough experience I have grown in strength to face the slings and arrows of the world. I have grown in compassion for myself and for others who suffered as I did.* The psychological work is grief over what was missing; the nonretaliation comes from spiritual awareness; the active compassion for others who suffer is saintliness. At this final level, our story and commitment are the story of the world, and our commitment is to universal compassion.

Today, as I write this chapter, it is Tisha B'av, a day of mourning for Jewish people. There is a national protest by Jews against the policies of the U.S. Immigration and Customs Enforcement. The news shows protestors carrying signs that read, "Never again" and "Close the Camps." They are relating what is happening now to refugees at our southern border to the death camps of World War II. The protestors today are recalling how their forebears suffered. Seeing the similarity is a psychological awareness. Feeling a caring connection is spiritual. The combination of awareness without vengefulness and action for others, not family related, who suffer abuse is an example of a saintly response. This also exemplifies how victims of the dark side might become champions of the light.

Nowadays we have a growing consciousness of childhood trauma. If this applies to us, it can serve as yet another pathway into knowing ourselves and becoming stronger. Sanity proceeds from as full a picture of ourselves as possible. Our response to our traumas requires a willingness to deepen our ownership of our story. To do this, we need to feel safe and secure. We can then chance an in-depth gaze at what happened, how we felt then, and what we feel now. In that context, we are more likely to confront the original trauma, process it, and resolve it with compassion for all the players—the path to genuine healing.

Past and present can become conflated. In the past we may have been powerless victims, yet we can only be powerless in the here and now if we are still living at the effect of the abuses of our past. Only if our original victimization is stunting our growth are we still victims. Our new description of ourselves is: once a victim; victim no more. We were victims when others had power over us; now we are self-empowered. In psychological health we remain traumatized but no longer call ourselves victims.

Traumas and events from childhood might also remain incomplete because we did not know the whole story of what was going on in our household. Family secrets definitely foreclose on any sense of completion. We might be hazy about what happened in the past or why we are triggered by it now. This does not harm us as long as we are not destabilized by our confusion. There is an element of "I don't know" in human life. We can respect that, while always remaining open to what we might discover.

We might also keep a trauma hidden from ourselves because facing it might mean admitting that we did not have parents who loved us. We would then feel like orphans, a much more terrifying option than awareness of the dismal facts. We might also avoid our psychological work by hiding what happened to us out of loyalty to our family. Our wounds are sometimes our only way to maintain our connection to our family. To become healthy is then configured as disloyalty because our agreed-upon role in the family is that of a victim. When we are included only if we are still "the dysfunctional one," the importance of inclusion might make us remain in our trauma. In this case, our role becomes crucial to our sense of safety: "I will be okay as long as I keep being the victim / problem person / caretaker / morale-builder."

I recall a client, Amelia, whose parents divorced when she was five. Her mother soon remarried, and she lived with three stepsisters until the age of ten. The stepsisters mistreated and ridiculed her relentlessly throughout those years. In fact, Amelia described herself as "Cinderella."

The stepsisters eventually moved to other states and had no contact with her. In one session I could see that Amelia was ready to dialogue with her past and asked her to bring photographs of each of the three to our next meeting. I propped up the photos on a table and asked her if she would be willing to address them one at a time about what they had done to her and how it had affected her. I suggested only that, intending to make another suggestion later. But to my gratified surprise, Amelia extended the interaction on her own. She ended each statement about herself and them with a kind wish that each of the three would now be having a good life.

In her dialogues Amelia showed no hate toward any of them. In fact, she said, "I hope you have learned to love others who are different from yourself. I hope others love you the same way." I ushered her into psychological work. Amelia elevated it to a spiritual, even saintly level. I was deeply impressed and told her so. Something strong and loving in Amelia's soul let go of the need to retaliate. That was a spiritual triumph. A deep, unconditional compassion also came through, a sign of saintliness. Amelia's therapy showed me how sanity, spirituality, and sanctity can happen simultaneously on the long path to the healing of trauma.

5

What Our Relationships Tell Us about Ourselves

It passes and we stay—
—EMILY DICKINSON, "A LIGHT EXISTS IN SPRING"

As Aldous Huxley was dying, his wife, Laura Huxley, recalled that her husband's last focus was, "How can I love you more?"[2] That is a psychologically healthy question when spoken as part of building intimacy in a relationship. It is a spiritual question when asked as part of loving a person and the world of persons. It is a saintly question when spoken at a highly charged time when most of us might be thinking only about ourselves.

Intimacy happens in a context of mental health when we give and receive love within a relationship. As we become more spiritually aware, we realize that we are here to expand our love experience until it contains the whole world. In saintly consciousness we believe we are continuously receiving divine love, and we do all we can to share this divine-personal love with the world around us.

Here are examples of psychological relationship issues that can open into spiritual practices and growth in holiness, the ultimate—and magnificent—purpose of all our human ventures.

---

[2] Laura Huxley, *This Timeless Moment: A Personal View of Aldous Huxley* (San Francisco: Mercury House, 1991), 117.

Needs

Needs are requirements for healthy development. We bring needs to our partner, and he or she brings needs to us. Our central love-needs might be summarized as attention, affection, appreciation, acceptance, and allowing. These five A's are the same needs we presented to our parents from our earliest days of life.

Demonstration of these five A's is a sign of true presence in a relationship. They also describe the essential components of love. When they happen between two people, they constitute intimacy. Let's consider each of them:

Attention: We ask for an engaged focus on our words, feelings, and experience. We also seek responsiveness to them. We want to be heard and seen for who we are. We want the other to show that he or she understands us. We want ongoing dialogue. When the other person is too caught up in him- or herself, the ability to focus on us is lacking. Only someone who can transcend one's own ego can be attentive. This shows that letting go of ego, a spiritual goal, helps us love. We needed attention in order to survive when we were infants. We need it throughout our life to thrive.

Affection: The human brain develops in early life through our frequent experiences of being played with, held, and cuddled. Our need for physical touch is therefore essential to our growth. We need physical holding with no sexual component in early life. In our adult relationships we seek physical holding with a sexual dimension, when it is appropriate. We need touch throughout our life, uninhibited but respectful of our boundaries.

Appreciation: To be appreciated is to be valued as precious to others. We need to know we matter. We wanted that from our parents. We want it now in our adult relationships. Appreciation is the opposite of being taken for granted or being treated as if we were invisible. We seek from others a sense of our importance to them. When we don't find it, we know instinctively that something we truly need is missing. This applies to all the five A's.

Acceptance: As we grow from infancy into childhood, we manifest a unique personality. Our need then is for full acceptance and approval of who we are turning out to be. We do not thrive when parents, or partners later, try to make us what they want us to be. Radical acceptance of us with all our light and dark dimensions is fundamental to a loving relationship. This acceptance gives us a sense of belonging—crucial to growth since we are social beings.

Allowing: Once we learned to walk on our own and no longer needed to be carried, we were beginning to show independence. We needed parents who could accept that. In healthy development we stay bonded to family but launch out on our own. We are doing this from the first day of school to the first day of independent living in the world as full-grown adults. In our adult relationships we want to be allowed to follow our own deepest needs, values, and wishes. We are already free as citizens, yet we need our freedom acknowledged and not infringed upon.

If, in childhood, we experienced the fulfillment of the five A's in a moderately reasonable—good enough—way, we are able to seek them ever after from others in *moderate* doses. When the five A's were not fulfilled, we might feel a bottomless pit inside and we seek too much—more than any other healthy human can, or is willing to, fulfill.

If we notice this excessive craving in ourselves, we can work on our childhood issues in therapy. We are committed to keeping our needs moderated rather than extreme or demanding. We are committed to expressing our needs and appreciating their fulfillment in a good enough way. We are willing to grieve any nonfulfillment in childhood and move on to self-parenting. We can then be ready for adult love from our partner.

This adult love can certainly include seeking a "mommy moment" or a "daddy moment" from a partner from time to time. Those are normal needs that can be fulfilled in a healthy way. But if we need parenting all the time, we don't have an adult relationship, only a parent-child one. Indeed, we never lose our need for fatherly and motherly love. It can take the form of caring, guiding, and supporting. We are not embarrassed to admit this need in ourselves. We are healthy when we seek it in supportive people around us. We are grateful to them when they offer it. We feel capable to offer it to others too.

Our spirituality is engaged when we can say yes unconditionally to the gifts and limitations our parents exhibited. We are open to the grace of forgiving. This follows naturally upon our psychological work of grieving the past and letting it go. We let go of ill will, resentment, blame, and the need to retaliate against our parents or any substitute person on whom we have transferred a father or mother face.

An effulgent spaciousness opens in our hearts. It happens because we let go of what we craved so desperately from others. Now we find it in ourselves *and* others. We find out how much space is in ourselves and in our life when what was crowding it out has finally vanished.

Holiness opens in us when we feel genuine compassion toward all those who suffer as we did. They become a focus of our caring, shown in action and in prayer for their healing. Our action might also take the form of special outreach to children who have been abused or neglected.

In all three phases of wholeness—sanity, spirituality, and sanctity—we can move from neediness to a sense of fulfillment. We can use this physio-psychological technique: We extend our hands at waist height, palms up. In one hand, we hold this affirmation and say it aloud: "I have needs." In the other hand, we hold this affirmation and say, "I have all I need." Holding that paradox has healing power. Here are three more sets of opposites. We can use this two-handed practice for each:

- From the psychologically healthy perspective, we acknowledge our needs and at the same time we trust our own inner resources. They save us from neediness, the must-have energy that turns others off.

- From the spiritual perspective, we have needs for a community of fellow practitioners, a sense of a divine accompanying presence. At the same time, we trust that all these are happening all the time.
- From the saintly perspective, we need the graces it takes to be dedicated to divine love, and at the same time, we always trust that we have them in abundance.

Problems with Closeness

Why do we withhold affection? Why do we fear getting close, emotionally or physically? What is scary about intimacy? Here are some possible answers:

- *We might not be able to trust the other with our vulnerability.* We believe the other might take advantage of it and use it against us later.
- *We might lose our freedom.* This may really mean that we can't trust ourselves to set the boundaries that will protect our own autonomy.
- *We might be engaging in retaliation against a partner who represents someone we were hurt by:* "I get back at my mother by distancing myself from my wife."
- *We might have been smothered with affection in childhood and now fear the same happening in our adult relationship.* We might have been constantly scrutinized and controlled by our mother or father or both. Now we equate closeness with those invasive behaviors. This certainly engenders anxiety about closeness.

Our psychological work can require visits to a therapist—on our own, as a couple, or both. On a self-help level, we also have some practices that might work:

- *We can foster emotional closeness by writing about our deepest feelings in the form of a letter to our partner.* We usually only give ourselves permission to do this on a birthday or on Valentine's Day, but we can do it on a monthly basis too. A warm part of us comes out when we sit alone and write. We find inner resources of safety that may not be so easy to access in ordinary daily behavior.
- *We can work through some of our physical fears by allowing closeness one more minute than we can stand.* As we do this repeatedly, we notice an exponential change in the direction of fearlessness.
- *We can directly ask for safety and security in how we share our feelings as we begin a conversation.* For instance, we agree that whatever we say will not be used against us later. Fear thrives in an unsafe, insecure atmosphere.
- *We can practice compassionate communication techniques that emphasize sharing about needs and letting any need be allowed, welcomed, and explored.*
- *We can each talk openly about the five A's*—attention, affection, appreciation, acceptance, allowing. We share how they were or were not shown to us in childhood. We share how we want them in our adult relationship. Our partner simply listens as a witness with no comment. We take turns. At the end, we hold hands in silent approval.

So far, we have learned that failures at being close stem from our early life. Thus, our work on ourselves psychologically is crucial to opening the door to spiritual and saintly loving-kindness. The wounds of childhood are trailheads into the full expression of our wholeness and holiness. Thus, hiking into the back country of childhood is a wholesome and holy venture toward closeness. We keep seeing how sanity, spirituality, and sanctity are interwoven.

Closeness on the spiritual plane is about self-sharing and openness to the sharing of another person. Yet, since spirituality involves *more*, we are sharing our feelings with a wider audience. We do this in ways that do not cross or interfere with the boundaries of others. We are simply more open across the board with the people we meet in the course of the day. Consequently, our openness to the feelings of others evolves into a caring about them, a spiritual practice. Our promise in any caring but respectful relationship might be, "I will never get too near but I will always be nearby." Thus, we address two main relationship fears, engulfment and abandonment: we promise neither to engulf nor to abandon the other.

Closeness becomes a saintly act when our compassion deepens not only for anyone in our daily life but for people everywhere. We engage in caring responsiveness to those who suffer anywhere in the world. We do this in whatever way fits our circumstances and personality. Regarding the plight of immigrants, for instance, we can show our concern on a wide spectrum: We can go to the border to offer support or join those where we are who are working to change policies. As an alternative, we can engage in prayer for the healing of those who suffer and for the conversion of those who cause suffering. All forms of a caring connection are acceptable offerings. We see this in the Hindu tradition when Krishna says, "Whatever someone gives me with devotion, be it a leaf, a flower, a fruit, or even water, I joyfully accept it as a love offering" (*Bhagavad Gita* 9.26).

Conflicts

All relationships are visited by a swarm of problems. Any relationship can improve with work on conflicts. We can take advantage of psychological tools such as addressing, processing, and resolving our issues:

- To *address* an issue is to confront it with no attempt to avoid its meaning, cover it up, deny its implications, or sugarcoat it. We are willing to call it by its name. We are willing to voice aloud what is troubling us.

- To *process* an issue is to experience the feelings that are attached to the original trauma or the present conflict. We also acknowledge that what we feel is connected to similar feelings in the past. We notice if we are profiling: women are like Mom; men are like Dad. We notice where in our body our feelings and sensations lodge.
- To *resolve* an issue is to come to a meeting of minds. It can also mean that we make an agreement to do things differently in the future. We let go of resentments about what happened. We avoid repeating the causes of the problem. All of this leads to a sense of closure, a feature of psychological health. We are reminded of a line from Walt Whitman: "The soothing sanity and blitheness of completion."[3]

Therapy or nurturant friendship can foster what British psychiatrist D. W. Winnicott called a "holding environment"—one in which someone holds a space so our feelings can be fully experienced, borne, and released. This is how healing happens through processing.

Gain from Pain

As we noted earlier, sometimes we remain in a painful relationship even though we have the power to change or exit it. In childhood we were victims of pain; in adulthood we may become volunteers for pain. For instance, we remain in an untenable relationship at home or work, we keep procrastinating about moving on with our own life, and we might maintain this stance because we are holding on to a self-defeating belief in powerlessness.

We might also be operating on the basis of an unconscious agenda. There might be some advantage to our pain. This is called a "secondary

---

[3] Walt Whitman, "An Ended Day," in *Leaves of Grass*, originally published in 1855.

gain" because we are benefiting from what is primarily negative. However, the "benefit" is ultimately not in our best interest.

We can ask, "What am I up to?" The answer will usually be fear-based. We may find out that we have a fear of getting on with life as full-grown adults. For instance, as long as we believe we are "unworthy," we don't have to do all we can to create a life that fosters our growth in self-esteem. "I am not good enough" is the slogan of a life that evades the challenges that can help us grow to our full human stature. Instead, we hold ourselves back, freeze-frame, and stay stuck. This is confusing—and depressing—to our psyche. We are contradicting our central human inclination to evolve, to step lively on life's journey.

The temptation for our family and friends is to make suggestions about how to change things for the better. We might then respond with "Yes, buts." We might also hear recommendations about how to build our self-confidence. Both these responses skip a crucial step. Our healing work begins with exploring the *gain dimension* of our behavior or thought pattern. What makes it safer to be stuck than to get on with life?

It helps to look into any self-negating messages from the past that are still posted on the walls of our body-heart-minds, still being obeyed. Such messages might even become the vocabulary of our own inner critic—that is, our self-incriminating, fear-based, shame-triggered voice.

As a psychological practice, recall a negative message from your inner critic. Notice how it points a finger of judgment at you, leading you to a sense of shame and powerlessness to do anything about it. List in a journal as many negative messages as you can. Beside each one, add a positive statement. You can ask for grace from the Holy Spirit of wisdom and love, the most powerful alternative voice to that of the inner critic. This combines psychological work with spiritual and saintly practice.

Here are examples of combining the negating and health-affirming statements. The first sentence is from the inner critic. The second sentence (in italics) is from the higher self or Holy Spirit:

- You don't know anything really. . . . *Like all humans, you are sometimes lacking in knowledge. I give you the gift of wisdom.*
- You will never be as good as the people you admire. . . . *Like all humans, you do not always match others in skill, but you are equal to everyone as a fellow human. I keep giving you unique gifts, and I help you notice them now.*
- You are a weakling. . . . *Like all humans, you are sometimes strong, sometimes weak. I give you the gift of fortitude and the grace to show it here and now.*
- You are worthless. . . . *Like all humans, you may sometimes feel worthless or unworthy. I value you immensely. I need your voice in the world, and it will be mine.*
- You are alone because no one really likes you. . . . *All humans are liked by some people and disliked by others. I am always with you and I hold you lovingly in my spacious heart.*

Make a commitment to yourself that, from now on, any statement from the inner critic will be followed by one from the Holy Spirit. This opens your interior dialogue to include all three S's of wholeness and holiness: sanity, spirituality, and saintliness.

Affirmations

As our work on ourselves progresses, we can create affirmations that cultivate deep change. For instance, we can, in the example of unworthiness, declare, "I am worthy of the best that life has to offer," "I appreciate my gifts and put them to use," "I accept my limitations and continue to stretch beyond them in any way I can," or "I let go of holding back and I now move on with confidence and joy."

These affirmations work best when we prefer a new next step to a lingering paralysis. More affirmations for self-esteem appear in chapter 8.

6

Healthy Sexuality

The way you degrade yourself into smallness is
abuse.

—RUPI KAUR, "THE SUN AND HER FLOWERS"

What is true in morality will always be health-affirming as well. Moral precepts are only legitimate when they are in keeping with physical and psychological wholesomeness. John Milton describes this succinctly in *Paradise Lost*: "God and Nature bid the same."[4] Thus, only what is physically healthy can be a wise spiritual practice.

Whipping ourselves is not a spiritual practice. Self-pleasure is not a sin. When we care about our bodies and enjoy them, we are honoring the divine life in human creation. We are listening to St. Paul: "Do you not know that your body is a temple of the Holy Spirit within you, which you have from God, and that you are not your own? . . . Therefore, glorify God in your body" (1 Cor 6:19–20). Self-care and joy in the full aliveness of body and mind are actually ways of honoring the divine creation of humanity. St. Irenaeus reminds us, "For the glory of God is the living man, and the life of man is the vision of God."[5] The word "vision" includes one's sexuality.

---

[4] John Milton, *Paradise Lost*, Book 6, 176, the John Milton Reading Room, Dartmouth College, online.

[5] See Irenaeus, *Against Heresies*, book IV, in *Ante-Nicene Fathers*, vol. 1, trans. Philip Schaff et al., chap. XXXIV, sec. 7.

Every human need, including sex, is entirely acceptable, part of being a body–heart–mind human. We also know, however, that any human appetite can become irrational or go out of control. Regarding sex, chastity as a virtue, therefore, means aligning our appetites with reason. St. Thomas Aquinas was once asked this intriguing question: "Was there sex in the Garden of Eden before Eve ate the forbidden fruit?" He replied, "Yes, of course, but without the compulsion and without the restlessness." His answer indicates what healthy sexuality is about. We engage in sex responsibly and with gusto. At the same time, we do not let ourselves fall into the traps inherent in the fulfillment of any appetite by becoming insatiable, obsessed, compulsive, or addicted, or trespassing over the boundaries of others.

The traditional understanding of chastity is abstinence from all forms of sexual pleasure. Nowadays we regard this as potentially dangerous to our physical and mental health, and antagonistic to our wholeness. Abstinence only works for specific periods of time, not as a lifelong practice. Chastity is not meant to be an ongoing repression but a condition or choice we sometimes experience. Chastity does not have to be about total abstinence from all acts of sexual pleasure. Likewise, chastity is ultimately about a fundamental commitment to something, not about occasional choices for the release of sexual tension. God does not call us to deny the body given to us, and that body includes a sexual dimension requiring attention and expression.

A thorough commitment to chastity can, however, be a choice for some individuals. It can mean that we do not want to be distracted from a singular and very absorbing focus on our calling. Chastity, then, can work as part of a relationship with God in which we reserve ourselves, for however long, to an apostolate that takes all our attentiveness. This is a special calling requiring a special grace.

We see this integrative challenge expressed by Thomas Merton: "It is precisely in the spirit of celebration, gratitude, and joy that true purity is found."[6] Likewise, we appreciate the integrated view in this definition from the *Catechism of the Catholic Church*: "Chastity means the successful integration of sexuality within the person and thus the inner unity of a person in his bodily and spiritual being" (§2337), a statement that beautifully combines wholeness and holiness.

Finally, we notice the double standard in our society regarding sexual behavior. When young men engage in promiscuity it is dubbed "sowing wild oats." When women do the same it is charged as "trashy." We also are aware that the male monotheistic religions are antifeminist—that is, in opposition to human equality. This appears so clearly in the first pages of the Bible. Original sin is imputed to Eve's eating the forbidden fruit. It is not attributed to Cain for committing fratricide. In the patriarchal view, men have wide leeway over life and death while women fall and cause falls by one quick bite.

---

[6] Thomas Merton, *Love and Living* (Boston: Mariner Books, 2002), 118.

7

Ten Steps to
Psychological Well-Being

A sound routine for staying alive on edges.
—Margaret Atwood, "Landcrab I"

The following steps enlarge and summarize what we have looked at in this part of the book so far.

1. *Maintaining a radical loyalty to reality.* As healthy adults we see and accept the givens of life. We accept the given limitations in ourselves and others. We appreciate our own and others' gifts. Our adult aspiration is a full acceptance of what is unchangeable, the courage to tackle what can be improved, and the wisdom to know the difference. For instance, we may work on finding what we need from a partner, then we realize that that person's capacity to fulfill us is beyond what he or she has to offer. We then reconcile ourselves to something less than we expected. We engage in realistic thinking, not wishful thinking. We redesign the relationship according to the resources available.

2. *Setting healthy goals.* We set reasonable goals for ourselves in all areas of our life. Examples might be psychological progress, excellence in sports, academic achievement, professional standing, artistic success, increasing resources, and so on. These goals are based on an honest assessment of our personalities, gifts, limitations, and capacities. We do all that it takes to fulfill our goals. We also try to exceed our goals whenever possible. We are not hobbled by failures. As body-heart-mind

beings we work for maximum bodily fitness, mental clarity, freedom of imagination, and emotional expressiveness. We increase our sense of our own self-worth as we notice our own fidelity to our goals and our skill at fulfilling them.

3. *Being free to be oneself.* We keep growing in self-esteem, self-caring, and self-compassion. We do not see ourselves as above or below others, only fellow companions on the human pilgrimage. We love showing ourselves just as we are. We are not people-pleasing but pleased to be with people just as we are. We want to present ourselves at our best, but we are not trying to look better than we are. Our enduring sense of humor allows us to laugh at ourselves and life's topsy-turvy turns. We act from a strong but humble ego, not an entitled or controlling one. We know ourselves as introverts or extraverts and act accordingly. We design our lives in accord with what is most important and valuable to us. We trust our gut feelings and our intuitive sense of ourselves, others, and life events. Our regrets have been transformed into grieving, amending, and letting go, rather than inner demons gnawing at us.

4. *Building a sense of personal power.* We let go of our fear of our own power. We do not believe that only people in authority hold legitimate power. We see obedience as necessary in society for good order, but we do not see obedience as an adult response to others' attempts at control over us. Our bodies, minds, and choices are not in the hands of "those who know better" or those who will punish us if we contradict their wishes. We are assertive, not passive. We act from choice, not obligation. Our lifestyle reflects our own needs and longings, while also honoring those of others. We balance our need for autonomy with our commitment to cooperation. Our boundaries are clear but also flexible.

5. *Expressing and receiving feelings.* We are comfortable with the full range of human feelings both in ourselves and others. We are not afraid to show our fear, courage, sadness, or joy. We have learned how to show anger in ways that do not include judging, blaming, or hurting others. Likewise, we can receive the feelings others might share

with us without flinching and without trying to talk others out of those feelings. We do not soft-pedal our own feelings so that others will like us. We do not sugarcoat the feelings of others so as to fend off their full impact. We do not use our feelings to manipulate others. We can stay present with others' feelings with compassion and openness to dialogue.

6. *Attending to our work/career.* We do what it takes to find the vocation, work, or career that reflects our talent, creativity, practical economic needs, and personal satisfaction. We are committed to being responsible about finances so that we can support ourselves and our families. We are honest in our work dealings with the public and at the workplace. We collaborate with our fellow workers. We have a sense of pride in our work, and in how we are advancing and what we are accomplishing. We keep looking for ways to make our work a vehicle to grow personally and to create a better world.

7. *Forming and maintaining effective relationships.* We want our relationships with an intimate partner, family, friends, and colleagues to be trustworthy and gratifying. This means being oneself and being able to be vulnerable. We display the five A's: attention, affection, appreciation, acceptance, and allowing. We deal with conflicts, problems, and concerns by addressing them directly. We do not deny or escape issues but face them. We process them by expressing our feelings and acknowledging our projections and transferences—that is, how what is happening in the relationship may hearken back to our early life. We look for ways to resolve conflicts with mutual understanding and reconciliation rather than prolong them by retaliation and estrangement. We honor the ground rules of all our various bonds.

8. *Celebrating our sexuality.* Our sexuality is an expression of an undeniable need in ourselves that is appropriate both while we are alone or with others. Our sexual choices proudly reflect our sexual orientation. Our sexuality is uninhibited and free of shame, while also being responsible and respectful of the boundaries of others. We are also alert to and clear about our own boundaries in our interactions

with others. The previous chapter on healthy sexuality explores other elements of this topic.

9. *Owning our dark side.* We are aware that we, like all humans, have what Carl Jung called a negative shadow side. It includes disowned and repressed antisocial impulses. We do not therefore believe that only "those other people" are capable of evil choices. We acknowledge our own capacity for acts and decisions that are harmful or unacceptable. We acknowledge that we can make the mistakes that any human might make. We see how we have hurt others and look for ways to make amends. We live by a commitment to act with integrity now and in the future. Yet, in humility, we stay on the lookout for any ways we might be choosing a path of malice. We look for ways we might be holding onto prejudices, and we do not act on them. We act with honesty in all our dealings. We do not deliberately hurt, harm, or hate anyone.

10. *Growing in social awareness.* We cultivate a civil and social sense that takes us beyond our own concerns. We genuinely care about our local community and its needs. Pope Francis in *Laudato Si'* wrote, "Our goal is . . . to dare to turn what is happening to the world into our own personal suffering and thus to discover what each of us can do about it." Thus, we are moved by the predicament of the planet *personally.* We are moved by the plight of those who are marginalized and oppressed. We look for compassionate ways to respond. We do not simply feel compassion for injustice but take a stand against the structures that create and perpetuate it. We do this in the manner that fits our calling and personality. It can be anything from radical civil disobedience to volunteering in a soup kitchen to sending a letter to a senator. Each of the three options requires a different personality; each is equally valuable.

> *We are spiritual beings who need love as much as we need food. . . .*
> *Survival of the Most Loving is the only ethic that will ensure not only*
> *a healthy personal life but also a healthy planet.*
> —Bruce H. Lipton, *The Biology of Belief*

8

Affirmations for
Sanity and Self-Esteem

Each of our sections on sanity, spirituality, and sanctity ends with affirmations. These are declarations that are carefully designed to bring us to the fulfillment of each of our three goals toward wholeness and holiness. Repeat any or all of these each day, aloud or silently. Allow any feelings that arise. Implement whichever ones you choose to work on in your daily life. Write on cards any that strike you strongly and keep them where you can see them during the day and then repeat them often. Be open and responsive to situations and events that test them—which will surely come along.

> I love and accept myself just as I am.
> I have a right to happiness.
> I am constantly growing into the full stature of my
>   adult self.
> I see my dark side and find ways to turn it into
>   creative goodness.
> I take responsibility for working on whatever in
>   me is ready for change.
> I keep finding new ways to let love enter my life.
> Every chaos in my life completes itself in peace.
> I feel harmony within myself.
> I see through and smile at the rationalizations that
>   keep me tied to old habits and fears.

I let go of my expectations of how I want things
    to be and I accept life as it is.

I choose reality again and again.

I let go of my compulsion to have more or to get
    more.

I use things and possessions without living in ser-
    vitude to them.

I let go of the need for approval from any man or
    woman.

I let go of my fear of any man or woman.

I am happy when people see me as I am.

I am complete, even when things are falling apart.

I have ever-surprising powers of self-restoration.

I accept my losses in life and I grieve them.

I choose to know and show my feelings.

I am clear to others and to myself about my
    choices, my agenda, and my motives.

My relationships are becoming more sane and
    healthy.

I ask for what I want, and I let go of the need to
    force people to give me what I want.

I drop control and let the chips fall where they
    may.

I show love, and it comes back to me.

I show forgiveness and feel my heart expand.

I trust myself to receive love and handle hurt.

I trust myself to receive loyalty and handle betrayal.

I let some people get close and I let others go.

I love myself and share my love with others.

I love to give and receive.

I show my vulnerability.

I let go of the belief that I am a victim.

I let go of the fear-based need to keep everything
the same.

I accept the given that there will be empty times
in my life.

I trust myself to know when to take hold and
when to let go.

There is always and already a serene sense of self-
assurance in my heart.

I make choices that honor true love and build self-
esteem.

I care about my community and contribute to it.

I welcome my time to win, to give in, to have, to
let go, to make my mark, to fight, to surrender, to find a foothold, to enter a void, to
dissolve, to stay, and to go.

I trust I have all the graces I need to be sane, spiritual, and saintly.

PART TWO

SPIRITUALITY

9

What Is Spirituality?

*Two people have been living in you all your life.
One is the ego, garrulous, demanding, hysterical,
calculating; the other is the hidden spiritual being,
whose still voice of wisdom you have only rarely
heard or attended to. As you listen more and more to
the teachings, contemplate them, and integrate them
into your life, your inner voice . . . is awakened and
strengthened, and you start to begin to distinguish
between its guidance and the various clamorous and
enthralling voices of the ego.*

—SOGYAL RINPOCHE,
THE TIBETAN BOOK OF LIVING AND DYING

As we noted in our introduction, in the faith perspective, support for
our growth in sanity, spirituality, and sanctity comes from grace—
from beyond our ego. It is described perfectly in the book *Alcoholics
Anonymous:* "With few exceptions, our members find that they have
tapped an *unsuspected inner resource* which they presently identify with
their own conception of a Power greater than themselves."[1] Thus, by
grace, we come to experience the realization of mystics the world
over: to find ourselves is to find God. To locate inner resources *is* to
discover divine graces. In the depth of humanness is something more

---

[1] Alcoholics Anonymous World Services, *Alcoholics Anonymous*, 4th ed. (New
York: AAWS, 2001), 307.

than we guessed, the life-spring of the divine. Essentially, spirituality is a consciousness of something more in us and in the universe. We see more in us than mere sanity. We commit to more than just psychological health.

The fact of "more" is what gives life depth and meaning. The more is not scarce; it is under any rock, in any shell, behind any star. For example, we notice that a symbol is more than what it looks like and that very "more" is what gives it depth and meaning. A poem does more with words than prose can do. Singing makes the voice shine more effectively than speaking, and dancing portrays movement more artistically than walking. A flag transcends cloth. Poems transcend language. "More" means transcendence, so we are in the realm of the spiritual.

The word "more" is not used additively, as in three is more than two. More, as a description of spirituality, refers to taking two to the thousandth power. We recognize a breadth and bigness in ourselves, others, and the world. We see more in ourselves than just an ego. We become aware of our identity as more than what is recorded on our driver's license; we are drivers of evolution. *To see more is to see with depth. It is also to see with spiritual awareness. Spirituality is a depth experience of life.*

We can see the world as more than a place; it is a spacious home that calls on us to make it just, loving, and peaceful. We experience time as more than duration; it is an eternal now rather than a now sandwiched between a past and a future. We experience a sense of oneness with nature and the human community that activates our lively move into service, tending, caring. We find ourselves going beyond loving only our near and dear. We love all beings. Thus, with a sense of "more" we widen the range of our spiritual consciousness internally and our social consciousness externally.

Our capacity for the transcendent also allows us to glimpse reality beyond what we see. For instance, when we are looking at a redwood tree, we are struck with awe at its firm and graceful contours, its easy ascent into the welcoming sky. In such an awe-filled moment, we are seeing more than just a tree. The awe we feel is a religious response since it takes us to the transcendent. We are seeing something more than a scientist can define. To understand how this differs from ordinary vision, compare that moment of awe at an actual tree to looking at an image of a tree on a box of cigars. There we see only the image, not the more-than. We see a surface without an interior. We "miss the many-splendored thing"—what inspires our sense of wonder, the transcendent, the more.

In that transcendence, we might also feel "held" by the natural world around us. Charles Baudelaire expressed this mystical realization: "The natural world is a spiritual house. We walk through forests of physical things that are also spiritual things and they watch us affectionately." We read the same from John Muir: "When I reached the [Yosemite] valley, all the rocks seemed talkative, and more lovable than ever. They are dear friends, and have warm blood gushing through their granite flesh; and I love them with a love intensified by long and close companionship."[2]

The depths—the more—of our psyche and the depths of nature *are* the depth that is God—three in one. Saints have found this trinity of oneness, themselves, the world, and God. This is why they are so happy and love so intensely. They have let go of differences.

From a Jungian point of view, mythic and religious symbols colorfully show us the mystical oneness of God, self, and nature. The beauties of nature, the images in our dreams or in the art we produce or find appealing, all depict the internal structures of our own psyche and the interior more that we call God. Thus, images arising from within or coming to us from the library of human history are self-portraits and simultaneously icons of wholeness, that is, divine presence. Carl Jung, in "Answer to Job," states, "The religious need longs for wholeness and therefore lays hold of the images of wholeness offered by

---

[2] John Muir, excerpt from a letter to a friend, written in 1873, in *Steep Trails* (Berkeley, CA: Sierra Club Books, 1918), 9.

the unconscious, which, independently of the conscious mind, rise up from the depths of our psychic nature."[3]

Freedom of thought includes freedom of belief. Regarding theological doctrines, some religious people adhere to the official teachings of the church; others are more open to modern interpretations, including their own. Moral teachings, likewise, then become guidelines, not restrictions. In either style, our religious beliefs can be more than merely notional thoughts in our minds to which we mentally assent. They can awaken us and lead us along three ravishing spiritual paths. Following these paths is how beliefs become spiritually enlivening. Our beliefs can reveal us, call us, and comfort us.

Beliefs reveal us to ourselves. By what we believe about God, we can see what we really are. Each belief about God mirrors a quality of our higher Self. For instance, our belief in the Incarnation shows us our human–divine essence. We thereby free ourselves from a dualistic view of God and humans or of body and soul. Joseph Campbell, in *The Hero with a Thousand Faces*, quotes St. Simeon: "I am human by nature but God by grace."[4]

Our life is a journey, a pilgrimage, and the shrine we go to holds an image of our true nature, our deepest consciousness. For Christians, this is Christ alive in the world of now. Every statue of a saint is a refraction of each of our virtuous capacities. We are not looking at images; we are looking into mirrors. *This is how belief can depict our identity.*

Beliefs call us. Our belief that God cares for the world beckons us to follow the divine lead into how we too can care. Our sense of God-at-work in the world is a call to go and do likewise: "Be merciful as your Father is merciful" (Luke 6:36). Our belief in transubstantiation in the Eucharist is real when we see ourselves as the bread of spiritual

---

[3] C. G. Jung, "Answer to Job," in *Collected Works,* vol. 11, trans. R. F. C. Hull (Princeton, NJ: Princeton University Press, 1977), 469, para. 757.

[4] Joseph Campbell, *The Hero with a Thousand Faces* (Novato, CA: New World Library, 2008), 332.

nourishment for the world around us. Then the words "Go, the mass has ended" become a call to show our eucharistic identity abundantly.

These words are attributed to Meister Eckhart, "What good is it to me if Mary is full of grace if I am not full of grace too? What is it to me if the Creator brings forth his son if I do not also bring him forth in my lifetime and in my world? This then is the fullness of time: when the Son of God is begotten in us."[5] We can say that our belief in the Trinity is not complete until we, too, are a community of loving persons. To believe we are made in the image of God is to hear ourselves called to live in loving connection with all beings, the best good news. Likewise, the mysteries of Christ's life show us our spiritual destiny, to be transfigured, to suffer redemptively, to rise, to ascend. His life is a full description of powers and commitments awaiting us. *This is how belief depicts our life purpose.*

Beliefs comfort us. We find safety and security in our faith: We trust the presence of a good shepherd when we are lost in the dark. We feel consoled in the midst of change by a changeless presence. We feel an assisting force guiding and supporting us as we move along on our journey through all the twists and turns of our life. We feel held by powers that have a caring connection to us. For instance, our belief that Mary is our mother means that we can trust and take refuge in a maternal affection that is all around us all our lives. We are finding comfort in the divine feminine that is inestimable in value and unending in reliability. *This is how belief depicts our spiritual foundation.*

---

[5] Meister Eckhart, "Be Mothers of God," Catholic Storeroom website.

10

Our Heroic Journey

I have a journey, sir, shortly to go;
My master calls me, I must not say no.
—WILLIAM SHAKESPEARE, *KING LEAR* V.3.340

A hero or heroine is someone who has lived through pain, been transformed by it, shared its gifts with others, and recognized all of the journey as attended by grace. In other words, our journey is to full-fledged spirituality.

The heroic journey has three phases: leaving, struggling, finding/sharing.

1. *We leave where we are and go somewhere new.* We are responding to a call to move beyond the familiar, the staid, and safe. We venture out beyond those limits to the more. Psychologically, going away from what is safe and secure is usually quite destabilizing. We feel anxious because we are forsaking the familiar. We are trying on a new style of being, not knowing what it will look like as it evolves. This stepping into the unknown can trigger anxiety, the opposite of safety and security. But this kind of anxiety also helps us. It shows us our need to access resources beyond ourselves. It moves us to make connections. We become humble enough to ask for help. We engage in spiritual practices. We begin to feel that we are accompanied by friendly spiritual forces that are on our side and at our side. In the Twenty-third Psalm, David walks through the dark valley and can sense a presence

accompanying him. This frees him from the anxiety he feels in the dim and dangerous hollow.

2. *We struggle as we encounter conflicts.* We don't let the forces that oppose our journey stop us. We also encounter assisting forces that help us and endow us with more resources. The incarnate Jesus is the divine assisting force. In the Letter to the Hebrews, we read, "Because he himself was tested by what he suffered, he is able to help those who are being tested" (2:18). Christ is able to help us on our journey because he lived through suffering and thereby helps us face and bear it. In our own lives, a painful psychological condition such as addiction can lead to recovery, redemption, and then to compassion for other addicts. This is an example of how personal suffering can become valuable and redemptive for all of us—the heroic style. Likewise, when we see a redemptive value in suffering, we are discovering the more in it, a spiritual realization.

Journey does not preclude pause, silence, inaction, or a dark night in which we lie in stillness and *wait* for what comes next. A period of powerlessness on the journey is not a cause of despair or a sign that nothing is happening. This time of immobility is not stuckness. It is not hesitation or reluctance. It is incubation, hibernation while we gather new powers—as happened in our mute nine months in the womb. It is likewise a cue to trust forces beyond, more than, the get-it-done ego. We show a reliance on a higher power rather than our so-often undependable selves. This power, this grace, conducts us through our powerlessness to the next phase of the journey. Examples of this period of quiet are Christ in the wilderness for forty days or the Israelites in the desert for forty years. Each was the prelude to a mission. Each was the necessary dark time in which the true bread rises so that it can nourish us and others.

3. *We find and share.* Ultimately, we find a gift that is always so much more than what was defined as our original goal. For instance, we go to Alcoholics Anonymous to stop drinking, but we find more, a whole new personality, one much better suited to self-realization. We don't stop at that. We take another step; we bring the message of

hope to others, the Twelfth Step of the program. Thus, our journey is about living through pain and helping others because of what we have gone through. We share the gift we have found. We show gratitude to a higher power than our ego for the graces that supported us in finding it. "We are ambassadors for Christ, since God is making his appeal through us" (2 Cor 5:20).

Yet making the good news known is not only up to us. It is happening by divine will always and everywhere: "I will display my greatness and my holiness and make myself known in the eyes of many nations" (Ezek 38:23). The Holy Spirit is thus on a heroic journey in every human heart and throughout the universe. She gives the power and makes us the witnesses of it: "You will receive power when the Holy Spirit has come upon you; and you will be my witnesses in Jerusalem, in all Judea and Samaria, and to the ends of the earth" (Acts 1:8).

A journey is not only external. Perhaps the next walk or journey we take will not involve a physical move. It might take the form of a new relationship or a career change. It can be a new intention to live by, a new set of values, and a new sense of self. A recovery program, for example, requires no physical move but definitely movement from addiction to sanity and spirituality.

Here are four Gospel examples of the more and how they help us to appreciate what the spiritual journey entails:

• *Matthew 10:31:* "So do not be afraid; you are of *more* value than many sparrows."

Psychologically healthy people grow in self-esteem. They see that they are worth more than what others may estimate or more than what their inner critic may cackle to them. They believe they are worthy of human and divine love. This inner assurance frees them from fear and sets them on their spiritual life journey. We recall St. Benedict in his "Prologue to the Rule": "See how the Lord in his love shows us the way of life."[6]

---

[6] St. Benedict, *RB 1980: The Rule of St. Benedict in English*, ed. Timothy Fry et al. (Collegeville, MN: Liturgical Press, 1981), prologue no. 20, p. 16.

• *Mark 12:33:* "To love him with all the heart, and with all the understanding, and with all the strength, and to love one's neighbor as oneself—this is much *more* important than all whole burnt offerings and sacrifices."

To love more is the central goal of a spiritually awakened person. This love is directed to God, a higher power than ego, the life-animating Holy Spirit ever-present in and among us. This love is also directed to ourselves and others. It is worth more than ritual acts. We were made for love and because of love. We can therefore trust that our capacity to love is boundless.

• *Luke 12:48:* "From everyone to whom much has been given, much will be required; and from the one to whom much has been entrusted, even *more* will be demanded."

A spiritually conscious person recognizes the gifts and talents entrusted to her or him. They are not simply givens of one's personality; they are meant to be invested in the service of humanity—a spiritual practice. This leads us to more awareness of why we are here. A divine presence in the world is asking us for more than we were given. We are here to find ever-novel ways to make our contribution. It is an over-the-top challenge, but grace is always available to support us. In fact, more is asked of us precisely so that we can trust and be thankful for grace, the source of all the more.

• *John 16:12:* "I still have many things *[more]* to say to you, but you cannot bear them now."

Essential to spirituality is an awareness that we don't know it all—and can't. We are living in a world of mystery—puzzling and dazzling. We have minds that can know the far reaches of spiritual reality only in part. Thus, our task is to open continually to whatever piecemeal communication waits to be transmitted. We will hear whatever of it we are ready for. This means surrender of our search-tooled minds to an inscrutable timing. We can trust that we will learn whatever of the divine-human reality we become ready for. We will learn the topography of our path but only gradually. That path is *more* than a yellow-brick road we can easily follow. It is, most often, a dark, unlit forest with no clearly marked trail other than the one we guess is there, or rather, here. We hear this from Emily Dickinson, in her poem "The Outer from the Inner":

> The Star's whole Secret—in the Lake—
> Eyes were not meant to know.[7]

Finally, we notice the word "more" used twice in the following quotation by Teilhard de Chardin. He shows us there is something more afoot than just our own work: "What fascinates me in life is being able to collaborate in a task, a reality, more durable than myself. . . . If death attacks me, it leaves untouched these causes, and ideas and realities, more solid and precious than myself."[8]

---

[7] Emily Dickinson, "Poem no 451," in *The Complete Poems of Emily Dickinson,* ed. Martha Dickinson Bianchi (Boston: Little, Brown & Company, 1929).

[8] Pierre Teilhard de Chardin, *The Making of a Mind: Letters from a Soldier-Priest, 1914–1919,* trans. Rene Hague (New York: Harper & Row, 1965), 144.

11

Two Spiritual Paths

There are two types of spiritual practice, formal and informal. By "formal" we mean following a specific method, virtually unchanging, usually from a trusted religious tradition. By "informal," we mean a spirituality that is personally designed, a set of views and practices, ever varying, that we gather from many sources or invent on our own. In both instances, there is a consistent and ongoing commitment.

The formal spiritual style can be based on the teachings of the Gospels or on the work of a spiritual teacher. In the Catholic tradition, St. Francis de Sales, St. Ignatius, St. Teresa, or any other recognized spiritual guide comes to mind. This style of spirituality includes being religious—that is, partaking of the sacraments and being connected to a faith community.

Here we focus on forming an individually designed spiritual program. At the same time, we draw from many traditions, especially the Catholic-Christian perspective. In this spiritual style, we configure life to be more than a series of years on the planet. We see life as a way to be present on this earth redemptively, that is, as dedicated to the nonviolence that creates justice, peace, and love. We are appreciating the magnitude of our life calling. We are always aligning our actions with the teachings we cherish. In this Christian experience of spirituality, we live with a robust trust in grace. We believe the Spirit gives us inner guidance and encourages us to follow the divine will in all that we are and do. Indeed, Christian spirituality is not about what we do but about what God the Trinity is doing in us, co-creating, co-redeeming, co-loving.

To *co-create* is to join consciously in the evolutionary thrust of the universe—still and ever being created. We are ecologically aware, climate-change conscious, and devoted to the thriving of our planet. We dedicate ourselves to forming institutions that further our sane use of earth resources. Like Jacob, we acknowledge the world as holy: "How awesome is this place! This is none other than the house of God, and this is the gate of heaven" (Gen 28:17). Once we appreciate our planet as the body of God, we act in ways that contribute to its evolution toward more connectedness, more consciousness, and more creativity.

To *co-redeem* is to join Jesus in his redemptive purpose of establishing new ways of relating to one another with holy love, new conversations about achieving peace, and new structures of justice in society. The socially aware Jesus speaks to us: "'The Spirit of the Lord is upon me, because he has anointed me to bring good news to the poor. He has sent me to proclaim release to the captives and recovery of sight to the blind, to let the oppressed go free, to proclaim the year of the Lord's favor'" (Luke 4:18–21).

This vision of redemption encourages us. We feel called to have, in the world and for it, the same heart that Jesus keeps pointing to. It is a heart for those in need, those enslaved, those blinded by greed, hate, and ignorance. This here-and-now social responsiveness is our co-redemptive work. We hear the call in Isaiah: "I do not delight in the blood of bulls, or of lambs, or of goats. . . . Learn to do good; seek justice, rescue the oppressed, defend the orphan, plead for the widow" (Isa 1:11, 17). The Decree, "Our Mission Today," echoes this thought: "Our faith in Christ Jesus and our mission to proclaim the Gospel demand of us a commitment to promote justice and to enter into solidarity with the voiceless and the powerless."[9]

---

[9] See Decree 4: "Our Mission Today: The Service of Faith and the Promotion of Justice," *General Congregation 32* (1975), no. 42, in *Jesuit Life & Mission Today: The Decrees & Accompanying Documents of the 31st–35th General Congregations of the Society of Jesus,* ed. John W. Padberg (St. Louis: Institute of Jesuit Sources, 2009), 298–316.

To *join the Spirit of love* is to show our love not only to our near and dear but to people far and wide. We consecrate ourselves to follow Jesus's command that we love one another as he loved us, that is, in every gentle way and no matter how others treat us. When we show a caring connection to others and to our world, we are joining the Spirit of God that brooded over the waters at the beginning of time. When we love, we are joining the Spirit at the consummation of history when all shall be united in Christ's kingdom of universal love.

This is how the Trinity makes a personal appearance in daily human experience. We are here to help that happen more by our sanity, spirituality, and sanctity. At the same time, we listen to this message from St. Paul: "But we have this treasure in clay jars, so that it may be made clear that this extraordinary power belongs to God and does not come from us" (2 Cor 4:7). Humility is indeed the central virtue of Christian life. We trust the power of God-in-us *more* than our own strengths and talents. We trust grace as the power that does it all, but always working through, with, and in us.

In any spirituality, our daily life is centered in prayer, a placing of ourselves in the divine presence with gratitude for what has been and what is, with openness to what will be. It is not talking but close listening to God speaking in our interior sanctuary and then promptly responding. Gandhi was once asked which of his many programs and forms of social change worked best. He said without hesitation that it was his own "silent prayer." Sometimes our apostolate is prayer rather than project. Sometimes it is both.

What is the place of religion in this approach? Being on a spiritual path does not happen automatically when we are religious. A person can be religious and not spiritual. For example, one can go to church but not have a personal relationship to Christ or any sense of serving and aiding the world. In the informal style of spirituality, one can be spiritual but not religious. In the Christian formal style, they happen together and complement each other. Spirituality as *more* always means a spiritual orientation that carries us beyond simply being religious. The following table distinguishes the two.

Religious Only	Religious and Spiritual
We believe there is a God.	We believe that God is active in our lives here and now.
We attend a church.	We participate in a caring community, for example, one that welcomes rainbow people and focuses on social action.
We participate in the sacraments.	The sacraments activate us in the world and feed us at a deep level.
We pray for what we want.	We lead a prayerful life. Our life becomes a contemplative prayer.
We might still have prejudices that reflect our politics or family background.	Our practice has taken root so deeply that our prejudices are no longer up and running.
We might think of our religion as the true one and may look down on the religions of others.	We see other religions as meaningful. We find wisdom in all traditions while cherishing our own.
Our religious practices may become rote.	Our practices remain powerful influences in our life choices.
Our beliefs may not have been upgraded since childhood.	We are continually pondering theology and upgrading our beliefs, learning about spirituality, and designing new practices.
Our loyalty to our religion may be based on its being part of our family tradition or national background.	Our path is our own and we are faithful to it because it works today.
Our purpose may be feel-good: Our religion gives us comfort.	Our purpose is co-creating a new world: our religion and spirituality include both comfort and challenge.

In mature spirituality, we are ready both for comfort and challenge. In the Twenty-third Psalm we are comforted by the shepherding God who is always with us, no matter how dark our times become or how adrift we feel at any moment. When we are growing in the sense of *more* we begin to see the psalm as offering something beyond personal comfort. It presents also a personal challenge: "I am here so that I too can be a shepherding presence for others and the world." The comfort we find in the psalm is actually a portal into a challenge: Trust in God opens us to an invitation to be God in the world. We are here to be what the Good Shepherd is. What we receive from the Good Shepherd is what we are baptized to give to others, what we are "anointed" for. We know that "surely goodness and mercy" accompany our every shaky step. This connection between what comforts us on our spiritual path and what we are here to be or do applies to all our spiritual resources. We are continuously integrating, that is, bringing all we do to wholeness and holiness, the paths to empowered love.

> *To turn all that we possess into the channel of universal love becomes the business of our lives.*
> —THE QUAKER JOURNAL OF JOHN WOOLMAN

12

An Unconditional Yes

Adult faith is grounded in total allegiance to human conditions, in serene acknowledgment of the merciless laws of nature and the often more merciless choices of human beings, and in capacities for restoration and redemption. In other words, adult faith is grounded in our commitment to create lovingly alternative responses to every given and condition and our faith is grounded in the hope that this alternative history of life will indeed triumph in the end. Until that time we will continue to pray for the grace to remain faithful despite apparent failure, recognizing that while this way of life leads sometimes to scorn, derision, imprisonment, and the cross, it is the only alternative to the lock-step march of dominant history toward war and death.

—*The Catholic Agitator* (Spring 1991)

In religious terminology, the givens of life, what happens beyond our control, represent what is called the will of God. Since who we are is a here-and-now given, to say, "Thy will be done," is primarily to say yes to ourselves as we are. Our healthy psychology makes this likely, since it includes a sense of personal value and worthiness.

We grow in self-esteem *and* spiritual consciousness when we say, "Thy will be done," since God's will is precisely that we be who we are, what we were created as: "I praise you, for I am . . . wonderfully made" (Psalm 139:14). We feel approved not reproved for the givens in our personality and in those of our story. We appreciate the givens of innate talents. We accept the givens of inborn limits.

Thus, a thorough acceptance of ourselves and of life as it is unfolding is more than a good idea psychologically. It is an essential ingredient of a healthy spirituality. Our radical acceptance of who we are is a trustworthy spiritual path to who we are called to be. Then our body-mind energy, our spiritual aliveness, and our saintly destiny work together without effort on our part. We find it easier to practice mindful presence in the world without judging ourselves, without complaining about our predicament, without entertaining false expectations about what comes next. We have gained a perch in the floating world. "Yes" is that unfailing perch.

Synchronicity follows, the meaningful coincidence of what we bring, whom we meet, where we go, and what is happening in the moment. The meeting of our resources and the world's needs applies both to spirituality and sanctity. We hear from Janet Erskine Stuart, RSCJ, "It is always here and it is always now. All our raw material for sanctity is in the now just as it is."[10]

It is a spiritual feat to say yes to reality, to life as it is with all its trials and opportunities. We are saying yes to the difficult givens of life: impermanence, risk, hazards in our ventures, betrayals in our relationships, suffering in our story, and meeting up with the dark side of human nature in ourselves and others. These are "the things we cannot change." We can deny them, blame God or man for them, and fight them tooth and nail, but they stubbornly remain facts of everyone's life.

Our spiritual stance is an unconditional yes while praying for the grace to accept them, no matter what the cost. St. Paul also notes this challenging spiritual—and saintly—option: "I have learned to be content with whatever I have. I know what it is to have little, and I

---

[10] Helen Rosenthal, RSCJ, *Reflections of an RSCJ* (blog), July 12, 2014.

know what it is to have plenty. In any and all circumstances I have learned the secret of being well-fed and of going hungry, of having plenty and of being in need" (Phil 4:11–12).

Our yes to ourselves as we are, to others as they are, and to life as it is leads to serenity, spiritually and physically. We might then come to the following realizations:

- It was when I stopped arguing with the givens of my life that I felt my whole body open. It was then I realized that I was finally and joyously grounded. I knew this had happened precisely because I had pledged a radical loyalty to my own reality.
- I now understand that anything that can happen to anyone can happen to me. I do not claim any exemption. I greet whatever challenges come my way with an uncomplaining yes. Now I am noticing that my yes actually endows me with a courageous readiness to deal with any challenge.
- I am lost when my happiness relies on getting what I want. I am on track when my happiness depends on maintaining an attitude of yes to what I have with openness to the *more* that will come next.
- I realize I am not alone in a world of givens like these. All my fellow pilgrims face them too. And somehow, being part of that fellowship makes them not only bearable but welcome.
- Regarding our yes to what happens to us, let's now consider how this response relates to each of our three topics of sanity, spirituality, and sanctity: *Psychology* informs us that present happenings are opportunities to learn from our experience and do better next time.
- *Spiritual wisdom* shows us that everything that happens to us—no matter how difficult or discouraging—presents us with an opportunity to practice mindfulness and loving-kindness.
- *Sanctity* shows us a path in and through the labyrinth of all that is to an opportunity to find God-within-it-all by a thread called

Yes. Then all that happens is not only an opportunity but a graced beginning. We then "end in what All begins and ends in—Yes."[11]

We are also mindful that opportunities come with a string attached, to reuse our thread metaphor. By some form of synchronicity, two realities in human experience usually arrive together: opportunity and danger. We find a chance to grow, but guarding the door is a threatening watchdog. As St. Paul tells us, "A wide door for effective work has opened to me, and there are many adversaries" (1 Cor 16:9). Regardless, we can do what he did and walk right in.

The givens of life are not all negative. There are gloriously positive ones:

- We have a lifelong capacity for love and bliss.
- Our hopes are sometimes exceeded.
- We keep discovering unique gifts in ourselves.
- Luck comes our way from time to time, but grace all the time.
- Miracles of healing happen.
- Everything that happens to us is yet one more chance to change and grow.
- No matter how dark the shadows, there is a light trying and ready to come through.

In this context, I share in poetic form an experience of my own:

> After every collapse of resources, after so many ir-
> reparable mistakes,
>   when I find myself lying in the mire,
>   the possibility of a yes inevitably taps me on
>   the shoulder.

---

[11] Omar Khayyam, "Rubáiyát of Omar Khayyam," in *The Literature of All Nations and All Ages,* vol. 2, ed. Julian Hawthorne, John Russell Young, and John Porter Lamberton (Philadelphia: E. R. Du Mont, 1900), 209.

Sometimes this reminder to accept my own reality
    comes from a place I least expected.
Sometimes it is a shred of love for myself
    from my shredded self.
Such wonders renew me, restore me,
    and walk with me over the dun moonscape.

Then the natural sadness sewn into this unpredictable world of griefs becomes enormously fascinating:

I notice a widening of my range of personal feeling,
    a psychological achievement.
I notice a compassion for others' sufferings, a spiri-
    tual shift.
I notice an expansion of my heart so that everyone
    and every given
    has room in it, a saintly grace.
I have suddenly become a little light in all our
    dark,
an oasis in all our wilderness,
    a smile in the midst of all our worried grimaces.
Then I see the calming connection between a yes
    to reality
    and communion with the divine.
And I suddenly see the divine feminine as the
    entry into it.
It is Mother Mary who comes to me with her
    harboring and encouraging care.
Her "Let it be!" is after all a "Yes!"

There has never been a word for
How it feels to have a mother like you, Mary,
Breasting all my hungry hours,

Prizing every sigh and tear and smile.
You open what in me can never wholly close.
And someday you will lift me by my dying breath
To your all-welcoming heart.
I want my last word to be your name, Mary.
I shall be lost in your beaming gaze, your hospice,
       hosting eyes.

In your arms that ached for my company since time
       began
My every longing all at once will cease.

(My own mother will be standing beside us
Nodding her head in bliss
And waiting her turn.)

13

Showing Integrity and
Loving-Kindness

Our spirituality has to take concrete forms. Following are practical
ways we can express our spirituality through personal integrity and
loving-kindness. I've been developing this list since 1998, and I present
it here in its most recent form. I recommend focusing on one of the
following commitments each week:

> I am caring for my body by a healthy lifestyle. I am
> caring for my mind and spirit by psychologi-
> cal work on myself when needed and also by
> faithfulness to spiritual practices.
>
> I do my best to keep my word, honor commit-
> ments, and follow through on my agreed
> tasks.
>
> I am making every effort to abide by standards of
> rigorous honesty, truthfulness, and respect
> in all my dealings, no matter how others act
> toward me.
>
> I forgo taking advantage of anyone because of his
> or her neediness, misfortune, financial straits,
> and attachment to or idealizing of me. If I
> am in a position of power or authority I do
> not misuse it. My question is not, "What can

I get away with?" but, "What is the right
thing to do?"

I keep examining my conscience with true candor.
I take searching inventories not only about
how I may have harmed others but also
about how I may not have activated my
potentials or shared my gifts, how I may still
be holding on to prejudices or the need to
retaliate, and how I may still not be as loving,
inclusive, and open as I can be.

I appreciate positive feedback. I also welcome
any well-intentioned critique that shows
me where I might be less caring, less toler-
ant, and less open than I can be. When I am
shown up as a pretender or confronted about
being mean or inauthentic, I am not defen-
sive but I accept the information about the
work I have to do.

I am letting go of the need to keep up appearances
or to project a false or overly impressive
self-image. Now I want to appear as I am,
without pretense and no matter how unflat-
tering.

I am not trying to ingratiate myself with anyone
in order to get on his or her good side. Being loved for who I am has become more
important—and more interesting—than
upholding or advancing the ever-shaky status
of my ego.

As I say yes to the reality of who I am, with pride
in my gifts and unabashed awareness of my
limits, I notice that I can love myself and that
I become more lovable too.

I now measure my success by the steadfast love I
have to offer and not by how much I have
in the bank, how much I achieve in business,
how much status I have attained, or how
much power I have over others. The central—and most exhilarating—focus of my life
is to show my love in my unique way, here
and now, always and everywhere, no one
excluded.

I appreciate the ways others love me, no matter
how limited. I am letting go of expecting—
or demanding—that they love me exactly
as I want them to. At the same time, I can
always ask for the kind of love for which I
long.

I am learning to trust others when the record
shows they can be trusted while I, nonetheless, commit myself to being trustworthy
regardless of what others may do.

I remain open to reconciling with others after a
conflict. At the same time, I am learning to
release—with love and without blame—
those who show themselves to be unwilling
to relate to me respectfully. I accept, without
judgment, the given of sudden unexplained
absence or the silent treatment by others and
will not use those styles myself.

When a family member suddenly cuts off communication with me, I ask for dialogue so
that we can repair the rupture. If the person
refuses, I respect his or her choice while
remaining available for communication. On
my part, I choose not to ostracize family

members who have offended me, nor do I
join other family members in their boycott
against someone. When I encounter family
division, I grieve the situation and stay open
to reconciliation.

I am learning to be assertive by asking for what I
need or want. I ask without demand, expec-
tation, manipulation, or a sense of entitle-
ment. I show respect for the timing and
choices of others by accepting no for an
answer.

I respect the freedom of others, especially those
I love. I do not want to use any charms of
body, word, or mind to trick or deceive anyone. I want others to have what they want.
I am not trying to manipulate or intimidate
others into doing what I want them to do.

I do not knowingly hurt or intend to offend others. I act kindly toward others not to impress
them, win their approval, or obligate them,
but because I really am kind—or working on
it. If others fail to thank me or to return my
kindness, that does not prevent me from be-
having lovingly. When I fail at this—or at any
of these commitments—I can admit it, make
amends, and resolve to act differently next
time. Now I can say, "Oops!" and apologize
more easily and willingly when necessary.

If people occasionally hurt me, I can say, "Ouch!"
and ask to open a dialogue. I may ask for
amends but I can drop the topic if they are
not forthcoming. Regardless, I do not choose
to get even, hold grudges, keep a record of

wrongs, or hate anyone. "What goes around comes around" has become, "May whatever goes around come around so that it helps everyone learn and grow." I am thereby hoping for the transformation of others rather than a retaliation against them.

I am noticing that my capacity to forgive others— and myself—is expanding all the time. This has graced me with a sense of joy and liberation.

I do not let others abuse me and, internally, I want to interpret their harshness as coming from their own pain and as a sadly confused way of letting me know they need connection but don't know how to ask for it in healthy ways. I recognize this with concern, not with censure or scorn. I do not gloat over the sufferings or defeats of those who have hurt me. "It serves them right!" has changed to, "May this experience help them evolve."

I realize that I, like all humans, have repressed and disavowed some negative and positive parts of myself. I am discovering ways to uncover this shadow side of myself: My strong dislike of certain *negative* traits in others makes me ask if I have similar traits in myself. My strong admiration for the *positive* qualities in others reminds me to look for the same gifts in myself.

I have a sense of humor but not at the expense of others. I want to use humor to poke fun at human foibles, especially my own. I do not tell racist or biased jokes, nor do I listen to them. I do not engage in ridicule; mocking; put-downs; snide, derogatory, demeaning, or bigoted remarks; sarcasm; or comebacks. When others use hurtful humor toward me, I want to feel the pain in both of us and look for ways to bring more mutual respect into our communication.

I do not hold anyone in contempt. I do not laugh at people for their mistakes and misfortunes but look for ways to be understanding and supportive.

I do not try to embarrass someone by shaming or making that person look bad in front of other people.

No matter how busy or in a hurry I am, I choose to act with patience and attentiveness toward others rather than to be curt, abrupt, or dismissive.

I have come to accept that fear is a given of life, at least for me. But there is one thing to which I can commit myself: I will not let fear *stop* me from doing what I need to do or *drive* me to do what I don't want to do.

I am practicing ways to express my anger against unfairness directly and nonviolently rather than in abusive, bullying, threatening, blaming, out-of-control, vengeful, or passive ways.

I am less concerned with being right or insisting on my own point of view in a conversation or group project. I am now more apt to listen to and appreciate the contributions of others, while also sharing my own view in a collaborative dialogue.

I notice that there are people who are excluded
from the in-group. Rather than be comforted that I am still safely an insider, especially
by joining in gossiping about those excluded,
I sense the pain in being an outsider. Consequently, I can reach out and include everyone
in my circle of love, compassion, and respect.

In a group situation, when someone is shamed, hu-
miliated, or harshly criticized, I do not want
to be glad that the finger was not pointed at
me. Rather, I want to support the victim of
aggression by asking for a respectful tone in
the dialogue. I know that standing up for the
victim may turn the bully's fury on me, so I
am continually working on building up my
courage.

I look at other people and their choices with intel-
ligent discernment but without censure. I still
notice the shortcomings of others and myself,
but now I am beginning to see them as facts
to deal with rather than flaws to be ashamed
of or criticized. Accepting others as they are
has become more important than whether
they are what I want them to be.

I avoid criticizing, interfering, or giving advice that
is not specifically requested. I take care of
myself by staying away from those who use
this intrusive approach toward me, while still
holding them in my spiritual circle of loving-
kindness.

I am willing to participate in the harmless con-
ventions and social rituals that make others happy—for example, family dinners or

acknowledgment of birthdays. If a social or family situation begins to become toxic, I excuse myself politely.

I am less competitive in relationships at home and work and find happiness in cooperation and community. I shun situations in which my winning means that others lose in a humiliating way.

I do not allow the judgments or impressions of others to contaminate my personal relationships. As a mindfulness practice, I am relating to important people in my life based on my own experience, not on gossip by others. I ask the same of those close to me: *You are who you are to me because of how I experience you, and I ask that I be who I am to you because of how you experience me.* What people say cannot recruit us to abandon one another, although it can open a candid check-in about what others report.

I never give up believing in everyone's innate goodness and that being loved by me can contribute to bringing out that goodness.

In intimate bonds I honor equality, keep agreements, work on problems, and act in loving and trustworthy ways. My goal is not to use a relationship to gratify my ego but to dispossess myself of ego to gratify the relationship.

My partner—or prospective partner—and I can contemplate this list together. These commitments can become the ground rules of our relationship. With this as a prenuptial agree-

ment we have found the path to trusting one
another.

I want my sexual style to adhere to the same standards of integrity and loving-kindness that
apply in all areas of my life. More and more,
my sexuality expresses love, passion, and joy-
ful playfulness. I also remain committed to a
responsible adult style of relating and enjoy-
ing life.

Confronted with the suffering in the world, I do
not turn my eyes away, nor do I get stuck on
blaming God or humanity but simply ask,
"What then shall I do? What is the opportunity in this for my practice of loving-kindness?" I keep finding ways to respond, even if
they have to be minimal: "It is better to light
one candle than to curse the darkness."

I feel a caring concern for the world around me.
I look for ways to work for justice and
commit myself to nonviolence. I support
restorative rather than retributive justice. I
feel myself called to action by violations of
human rights, prejudice, hate crimes, gun
violence, genocide, nuclear armaments, economic injustice, and ecological exploitation. I
continue to educate myself on these issues.

With planetary consciousness, I tread with care on
the earth with what St. Bonaventure called "a
courtesy toward natural things."

I appreciate that whatever love or wisdom I may
have or show comes not *from* me but *through*
me. I give thanks for these encouraging

graces and say yes to the stirring call to live up to them.

These ideals are becoming my personal standards. I trust them as pathways to psychological and spiritual maturity.

I notice that each entry on this list empowers me: I feel stronger, more self-assured, more at home in the world, more able to handle whatever comes my way.

I am not hard on myself when I fail to live up to these ideals. I just keep practicing earnestly. The sincerity of my intention and my ongoing efforts feel like the equivalent of success. I am letting go of perfectionism and of guilt about not being perfect.

I do not think I am above other people because I honor this list, nor do I demand that others follow it.

I am sharing this list with those who are open to it.

I keep placing the intention—or praying—that someday these commitments can become the style not only of individuals but of groups in the world community: corporate, political, and religious.

14

Our Options
in the Face of
Hate or Hurt

*To our most bitter opponents we say: We shall match
your capacity to inflict suffering by our capacity to
endure suffering. We shall meet your physical force
with soul force. Do to us what you will, and we
shall continue to love you. We cannot in all good
conscience obey your unjust laws, because noncoop-
eration with evil is as much a moral obligation as
is cooperation with good. Throw us in jail, and we
shall still love you. Bomb our homes and threaten
our children, and we shall still love you. Send your
hooded perpetrators of violence into our communities
at the midnight hour and beat us and leave us half
dead, and we shall still love you. But be ye assured
that we will wear you down by our capacity to suffer. One day we shall win freedom, but not only
for ourselves. We shall so appeal to your heart and
conscience that we shall win you in the process, and
our victory will be a double victory.*

—Martin Luther King Jr.,
sermon delivered
at Dexter Avenue Baptist Church
in Montgomery, Alabama

At times, people may hurt our feelings, purposely or not. In psychological health, our response is "Ouch!" Then we open a conversation about our hurt and the grief it has triggered. We do this without blame, though we do ask for amends. We do not stay around for more abuse.

In spiritual consciousness, we open ourselves to the grace to reconcile, to let go of ill-will, resentment, and the need to retaliate. Spirituality thrives lavishly in an atmosphere of reconciliation and forgiveness.

In saintly commitment, we respond with kindness to those who hurt us, whether they apologize or not. Sanctity is always over the top, always entails more than what is expected. For a saint, nothing can happen that is not penetrable and forgivable by love.

Our motivation in psychological health is comity. Our motivation in spiritual awareness is community. Our motivation in sanctity is communion.

A spiritual or saintly commitment to reconciliation rather than punishment means that our compassion extends not only to victims of violence but also to its perpetrators. We can feel compassion for them equally but will choose to show it differently: We will comfort the victim and support him or her in speaking up and seeking redress. We will help the perpetrator find the needed help. Likewise, we will support civil programs of restorative justice rather than retributive punishment. We will put our energy into reconciling rather than punishing. We will build our capacity to forgive rather than our capacity to retaliate.

Here is a historical analogy. At Appomattox, Union soldiers began a one-hundred-gun salute to celebrate General Robert E. Lee's surrender of the South. General Ulysses S. Grant immediately ordered that it be stopped. He commented on that moment in his *Memoirs*: "The Confederates were now our prisoners and we did not want to exult over their downfall."[12] The soldiers were acting sanely. Grant was

---

[12]Ulysses S. Grant on April 9, 1865, in *Personal Memoirs of U. S. Grant* (1885; Boston: Belknap Press, 2017), 726.

acting with spiritual consciousness, compassion, and a lack of vengeful-ness toward the defeated.

In addition to having our feelings hurt, sometimes people hate us. We do not have to adopt the primitive reaction of retaliation. We have other options in the face of hate or hurt. Let's consider four possibilities:

A primitive reaction. Our reptilian brain is geared from cave-people days to hit back, to get even, and then some. In this attitude, we are visiting an uncivilized, unmissionized territory of our psyche. In that dark country, there is no Buddha, Christ, St. Francis, Gandhi, Martin Luther King Jr., Mother St. Teresa, or Dalai Lama. We can only design our behavior in mirror image to the meanness others have perpetrated on us; we hate or hurt them back. To make matters worse, when we are offended, we refuse to accept a sincere apology or repentance from the offender. We do not seek, desire, or even allow his or her redemption. We insist on punishment as the only consequence that clears the decks. Only the suffering of the offender can satisfy us. We may even apply this mean-spiritedness to our thoughts about the afterlife: We abhor Christ's call to sinners to repent. We want only eternal torture—the damnation—we believe they deserve.

Now we are using the street rule to "do as you are done by" and "pay for your crimes." We are fueled by adrenaline and testosterone, the main hormones of the indignant ego. We are stressed by how oth-ers treated us, and we increase our stress by biting the hook that ties us to ongoing feuding.

In this context, we meet anger—displeasure at injustice. It can coexist with love when we express it safely with an "Ouch!" but do not then become aggressive, retaliatory, or punitive. We simply com-municate our angry feeling nonviolently.

However, we are aware of a danger regarding how people show anger. There can be a power differential in its expression. When it hap-pens in a one-up/one-down relationship, the angry person allows him- or herself to become punitive or violent. For instance, in a hierarchical arrangement, an authority figure—someone who has assumed power over our well-being, freedom, and safety—has the right to punish us if we cross the one who is one-up. In egalitarian relationships, there is no penalty automatically associated with anger. In inequitable relationships—parent to child, boss to worker, court to citizen, criminal to victim—punishment in various forms becomes legitimate. We note, however, a spectrum here. A parental punishment is a harmless teaching device: "Take a time-out in your room." A civil punishment is a law-supported demand for restitution. A criminal punishment might be injurious. Healthy people show anger but do no harm.

A healthy psychological response. We feel grief about what happened. We report our pain at what the other did and look for a way to establish a dialogue. We express our hurt to that person directly. We also set boundaries so that we can protect ourselves from further attacks. This may mean no further contact, or it may mean moving together toward reconciliation. That will depend on how willing the person is to work things out with us. Regardless, we combine assertiveness about the impact of her or his behavior with receptiveness to a positive solution.

A spiritual response. We speak up, set boundaries, and remain open to dialogue, but we do not hate or hurt back. We follow the Golden Rule. We adhere to our ethical standard to treat all people with respect. We are not duplicating the aggressor's style. We design our own creative response to what happened. We keep in mind Michelle Obama's recommendation: "When they go low, we go high." We remain nonviolent throughout. We want a win-win situation, not one that triumphs over the aggressor. We notice we like ourselves more when we take this path. We also increase our self-esteem because we remain faithful to standards of assertiveness while at the same time holding a loving intention. Only psychologically healthy and spiritually committed people can effect that felicitous connection.

A saintly response. As with the spiritual response, we speak up, but we do not hate or hurt back. Then we go beyond the spiritual; we do *more.* We find a way to extend goodness to those who have hurt us. We try to win them over to a style of enlightened goodness by the example of our own unconditional love. We share our feelings about what happened, *and* we look for ways to let go and forgive. We combine the teachings of the Sermon on the Mount and Buddhist loving-kindness. We ask for the grace to be this way, and we are thankful for the grace of being this way.

Here is a summary of responses from sanity, spirituality, and sanctity with respect to forgiveness. This example helps us see how the sanity, spirituality, and saintliness can work together:

- The psychologically healthy person forgives when the other apologizes or makes amends.
- The spiritually adept person forgives whether the other is repentant or not.
- The saintly person forgives "seventy times seven."

All three have this in common: they are in favor of repentance and reconciliation rather than punishment.

Finally, once we are free of the need to exact revenge, we will find it difficult to believe in eternal torment. If the best part of us can forgive any hurt, we can believe that God has the same capacity. A spiritually aware person reads this statement of the fourteenth-century mystic Julian of Norwich with a sense of liberation: "Holy Church taught me that sinners are sometimes deserving of blame and wrath, but in my visions, I could not see this in God. . . . God is the goodness that cannot be wrathful . . . . I saw no vengeance in God not for short time nor for long. God shows us no more blame than he does to the angels in heaven. . . . I saw no wrath except in humans, and God forgives that in us."[13]

In addition, here are some spiritually mature teachings of St. Isaac of Syria, a seventh-century bishop who believed in universal

---

[13] See Julian of Norwich, *Revelations of Divine Love*, ch. 45.

reconciliation rather than eternal damnation: "God's recompense to sinners is that, instead of a just punishment, God rewards them with resurrection. . . . In the fire of love, our compassion extends even to the demons. . . . God chastises with love, not for the sake of revenge but to make whole his image. This is the aim of love. Love's chastisement is for correction not for retribution."[14]

> *Hell itself will pass away,*
> *And leave her dolorous mansions to the peering day.*
> —JOHN MILTON,
> "ON THE MORNING OF CHRIST'S NATIVITY"

---

[14] Adapted from Bishop Hilarion Alfeyev, *The Spiritual World of Isaac the Syrian, Cistercian Studies* vol. 175 (Collegeville, MN: Liturgical Press, 2000).

15

Ten Steps to Spiritual Growth

*The Christian does not learn a new set of unworldly
laws which he opposes to the ways of the world, but
by the Cross, the Love of Christ, and the indwelling Spirit of freedom, he learns to live in the world
as Christ did, in perfect liberty and with unlimited
compassion and service.*

—THOMAS MERTON, *LOVE AND LIVING*

These steps will summarize—and elaborate upon—what we have been
exploring in this part.

1. *Showing reverence to the natural world.* A sense of reverence toward
the wonders of nature is an experience of transcendence. We sing this
in the liturgy: "Heaven *and* earth are full of your glory." In the Bible,
the word "glory" refers to the divine. We look at nature with awe for
the divine rather than with avarice for how it can profit us. We honor
all that nature offers as nurturant and aesthetic. We do not look for
ways to exploit it. We are not rapacious but respectful. St. Francis is
an example of someone who saw nature as egalitarian rather than as
a hierarchy of humans ruling it for their gain.

2. *Letting go of ego.* When we let go of our self-centeredness, our
healthy ego remains, and our arrogant, inflated, entitled ego fades.
We are no longer demanding that others honor us as the center and
focus of their attention. We let go of trying to control others or gain
ascendancy over them. We see how much we have invested in being

in full control. We see our fear of the future as an indication of our self-doubt about our own power. Our worry is not about what might happen but about how we won't be able to be in full control of it. The opposite of control is yes to uncertainty. We let go of the belief that we deserve immunity from unpredictability, a given of life to which all beings have to bow.

3. *Increasing social consciousness in spiritual ways.* When we keep increasing our social consciousness, we transcend any religious spirituality that is about "God and me." Our spirituality has an apostolic intent, a sense of mission, and a sharing of good news and better actions. We grow in the realization that life is mainly about service to others rather than only about the fulfillment of our own ambitions. We are responsive to injustice. We look for ways to make our world a safe and peaceful place. We share good news by showing how powerfully it has worked in us, and we know it has worked when we have learned to love: "By this everyone will know that you are my disciples, if you have love for one another" (John 13:35).

4. *Befriending the shadow.* We are aware of the dark side in ourselves and in all people. We accept that fact but we transcend it too. We look for ways to integrate our shadow—befriend it—so that our creativity can emerge and lead us to paths of goodness. Darkness is never the last word when we are animated by faith. We begin to think more like Dorothy Day, who wrote, "No matter how corrupt the Church may become, it always carries within itself the seeds of its own regeneration."[15] We hold that same hope with regard to ourselves, others, and every human enterprise. The "seeds" are not the magic ones of Jack and the beanstalk. They are the ever-embraced opportunities to meet any rupture with repair. Regeneration of any relationship—individual to individual, institution to individual, or individual to institution—happens when we do all we can to mend what has been broken, even trust.

---

[15] Written to Karl Meyer, August 3, 1971, in Jim Forest, *All Is Grace: A Biography of Dorothy Day* (Maryknoll, NY: Orbis Books, 2011), 273.

5. *Liberating ourselves from duality.* Our sense of ourselves and others is free of dualism and separateness. *Our letting go of belief in an up-there, dualistic God is not a sign that we have lost our faith. It is a discovery of enlightenment.* We are then animated by a cosmic consciousness, an orientation to the arc of evolution. With this attitude we can enable others to grow in awareness of our oneness. We evolve with the universe toward more light, and a more caring connection. We see the entire universe as blooming with lively energy, what Gerard Manley Hopkins called "the dearest freshness deep down things."[16] We feel the same presence of love upholding each of us and the entire universe. We do all we can to further this amiable project.

6. *Holding adult beliefs.* We let go of superstition, wishful thinking, and practices that attempt to give us safety and security. We are now living as adults who have freed ourselves from irrational beliefs. We are grounded in reality. Our trust in grace has supplanted any fantasy that remaining in a religious institution promises, like sure-fire techniques to get our way in this life or in another. We do not regard providence as a promise that all will turn out as we want it. In mature spiritual consciousness, providence means that, no matter what happens, we will be able to find in it an opportunity for spiritual practice and virtue. Providence at its best guarantees that no power on earth can cancel our capacity to love.

7. *Being faithful to spiritual practices.* We engage in spiritual practices such as meditation, prayer, contemplation, affirmations, and meaningful rituals. We maintain a daily commitment to our practices. Our sincerity in and faithfulness to these practices is comforting and edifying. At the same time, they also challenge us. For instance, we feel ourselves emboldened to stand up for nonviolence as the path to social change, joining so many spiritually aware people both from the past and in the present.

---

[16] Gerard Manley Hopkins, "God's Grandeur," in *Gerard Manley Hopkins: Poems and Prose* (New York: Penguin Classics, 1985).

8. *Choosing virtuous ways of living.* We are committed to rigorous honesty and integrity in all our dealings. The Tibetan Buddhist teacher Chögyam Trungpa reminds us, "The practice of meditation is not so much about the hypothetical attainment of enlightenment, but with leading a good life."[17] This "good life" means following the golden rule as a spiritual practice whether others follow it too, or not. We adhere to a spiritual standard because we have adopted it as our path, irrespective of how others behave. We act in accord with a set of spiritual values and do not copy what others may do.

9. *Showing loving-kindness.* We practice loving-kindness toward all human beings. We begin with ourselves, then those close to us, then those who are neutral to us, then those with whom we are in conflict, and finally to all people everywhere. All that we do in any spiritual practice leads us to an unreserved love, our life purpose, the richest grace we can receive or share. We gladly and frequently exhibit the five A's: attention, affection, appreciation, acceptance, and allowing. We see love as our central spiritual practice and do all we can to show it everywhere. At times, we may fail, but we maintain the purity of our loving intention.

10. *Staying aware of grace.* We are always aware of the need for help from a higher power than our ego. We feel ourselves held and supported by many assisting forces, seen and unseen. Some are other humans around us now. Others have gone before us. These supportive presences, in Christian theology, make up what is called the Communion of Saints, which we will explore in part III. We can believe in assistance from our ancestors, saints, bodhisattvas—in Buddhist tradition, enlightened beings who help us. We can believe that the spiritual people who have passed away still care about us, and we can call upon them for guidance. We are grateful for their help. A touching hymn of St. John Chrysostom to Mary on the feast of her Assumption says, "You went away but never left us."

---

[17] Chögyam Trungpa, *The Path of Individual Liberation: The Profound Treasury of the Ocean of Dharma,* vol. 1, ed. Judith L. Lief (Boulder, CO: Shambhala, 2014), 228.

16

Affirmations for Spiritual Progress

Use these affirmations daily to foster a spiritual consciousness and support a spiritual program of action in your daily life. They state the truth of who you are spiritually. They seem beyond our reach, but repeating them makes them real for us.

> I show more love than ever.
> I listen carefully to what the universe and others
>   tell me about myself.
> I acknowledge access to powers beyond my ego-
>   mind.
> Something wonderful lives on in and through me.
> I feel an unconditional, inalienable, and indestruc-
>   tible love within and around me.
> I keep finding the prize of perfect awakening.
> My present predicament is full of wisdom.
> I continually notice and am thankful for the spiri-
>   tual shifts that keep happening within me.
> I show my unconditional love and wholeness in
>   my every thought, word, and deed.
> I feel spiritual abundance in my heart.
> I shower spiritual abundance upon the world
>   around me.
> I am on a journey that takes me through pain to
>   transformation.

I trust my inner voice.

I am thankful for the assisting powers accessible to me always and everywhere.

I acknowledge my destiny to show in my lifetime the timeless love within me.

I embrace my destiny to articulate the eternal wisdom within me here and now.

I let the imperishable rose of wholeness bloom within me.

I have an identity that transcends my personality.

I choose to show love repeatedly to everyone, now and ever.

I began in love and live in love until the end.

I feel the joy of loving.

I feel the joy of giving.

I feel the joy of receiving.

I accept the givens of life.

I let go of the belief that the conditions of life will be repealed for me.

I let go of the belief that things will always be fair.

I let go of the belief that things will always be clear.

I let go of the belief that things will always be predictable.

I let go of the belief that things will be as I want them.

I accept the givens of life with appropriate grief and radical trust.

I am thankful to be finding grace everywhere.

I trust that I have all the graces necessary to be sane, spiritual, and saintly.

PART THREE

SANCTITY

17

What Is Sanctity?

*I have been disillusioned, however, this long, long
time in the means used by any but the saints to live
in this world God has made for us.*

—DOROTHY DAY, "ON PILGRIMAGE"

Sooner or later we realize, with exceeding joy, that spirituality and
all our spiritual practices form a sturdy bridge to our final goal of
wholeness and holiness.

Let's begin by considering our three topics and some simple de-
scriptions:

Sanity is enough. It is sufficient, for a psychologically satisfying life.

Spirituality is more. It takes us to more than that, to a dedicated
presence in a world alive with the divine. It is not a final goal; it is
incomplete in itself. Spirituality is a *threshold* to sanctity, the true and
final fulfillment of all we could ever be.

Sanctity is most. It expands the possibilities beyond the spiritual
more into a relationship with the divine More through contemplation and Christ-like love of others. This means activating the most we
are capable of, a selfless, focused, and caring commitment to service
in our evolving world. All of us are heirs to the graces that can make
this happen.

Wholeness happens in a context of sane living and spiritual consciousness. Holiness happens in saintly living and heroic action. All this
can come to pass in our ordinary day-to-day world. Indeed, the world

of spirituality and sanctity is not up in the sky, nor is it disembodied in any way. It happens every day on this earth. St. Irenaeus wrote, "Christ did not despise or evade any condition of humanity, nor set aside for himself the law which he had appointed for the human race, but sanctified every age."[1] In other words, he said yes to the givens of life rather than ask for a reprieve from them. In fact, the givens of human existence, including death, are the very conditions from which redemption arises.

We have heard or said, "I am not a saint." Usually, this means, "Don't expect me to be perfect." But a saint is not perfect in the sense of being totally saintly every minute of every day. Such consistency is not possible for humans in any area of life. A saint is an ordinary person who is animated by an extraordinary love. A saint is also someone dedicated to and focused on the issues that make love concrete. Thus, Ruth Bader Ginsburg is a saint for human rights as are Jimmy Carter and the Dalai Lama. Likewise, all people who, in their own big or little way, show caring for justice, peace, and love are saints too. A saint does not have to have died. There are many living saints, the assisting forces in our generation.

We go through an ordinary day in ordinary ways, making some mistakes, not always on tap for saintly action but always holding a pure intention to be as loving and as committed to service as we can be. That is sanctity. The purity of our dedication is the equivalent of perfect fulfillment.

Likewise, in special moments—not all the time, but when the world needs us in some especially challenging way—we step up to the plate, however gingerly. We may do this with eagerness and readiness or with fear and trembling. But either way, we do the best we can. We see the needs of the world as God appearing to us in person and we respond with generosity and loving-kindness.

Here are some general qualities of sanctity. Each saint is unique, so the entire list does not necessarily apply to every saint:

---

[1] St. Irenaeus, *Against Heresies* 2.22.4.

- A saint says yes unconditionally to the givens of life, the "will of God," because he is yes: "In him [Jesus] it is always 'Yes'" (2 Cor 1:19).
- A saint says yes unconditionally to the voice of the Holy Spirit speaking personally to his or her conscience.
- A saint experiences the sacred in all that is. A saint feels the "more," the transcendent dimension in all as divine presence. For a saint, reality itself is holy. Any form of dualism is recognized as illusion.
- A saint lives out what he or she believes. A saint walks the talk.
- A saint is focused on a single-hearted sense of mission and is willing to make sacrifices for its fulfillment.
- A saint is free from attachment to worldly ties so that life can be primarily geared to service.
- A saint is satisfied with progress, not perfection.
- A saint practices unconditional and universal love for self, others, and all beings.
- A saint is free of bias and hate. A saint is not racist, homophobic, and antifeminist. A saint is not against religious or political freedom, nor is she or he elitist or divisive in any way.
- A saint suffers with the oppressed and prays or works for their liberation.
- A saint looks for ways to change whatever perpetuates injustice in a social system, either through prayer or action or both. Not all saints engage in social action, but all saints care about the wider world.
- A saint practices the works of mercy as a form of prayer. Dorothy Day said, "Our rule is the works of mercy. . . . It is the way of sacrifice, worship, a sense of reverence."[2]

---

[2] Jim Forest, "The Catholic Worker Movement," in *Encyclopedia of American Catholic History,* ed. Michael Glazier and Thomas J. Shelley (Collegeville, MN: Liturgical Press, 1997), 310.

- A saint is a prophetic witness, one willing to look at what is happening and call it out if it is unjust.
- A saint is committed to nonviolence in his personal and political actions. He believes this is the only path to a world of justice, peace, and love.
- A saint never knowingly retaliates, no matter what the provocation, nor does he or she support laws and policies that sanction torture or war.
- A saint defies and reverses the values of the establishment. A saint lives life upside-down.
- A saint is dedicated to sharing, and says, "All the joys and growth I find, I want all beings to find too. All I find is for all."
- A saint may exert enormous effort in spiritual practices yet experience progress in the spiritual life as the result of grace, not effort; gift, not reward. A saint does not seek merit or recompense only the joy of furthering the reign of eternal goodness.
- A saint has equanimity in the face of danger, threat, and triggers. This shows the depth of his or her personal relationship with God.
- A saint has a deeply personal relationship with God, based on an experience of God.
- A saint feels accompanied no matter how dark the inner night may become or how comfortless life and spiritual practice may be. For a saint, a dark night of the soul is a path, not an avalanche; a bidding, not a halting.
- A saint regularly practices some form of contemplation, meditation, prayer, or interior silence or devotion.
- A saint's calling may no longer feel like a choice. A saint can't help but make God's work the center and circumference of his or her life.
- A saint lives in communion with all that is, and all that is *is* God.
- A saint is ready for the call to be heroic if that challenge presents itself. St. Oscar Romero stayed put when he knew that to do

so would mean martyrdom. Mother St. Teresa stayed faithful to the poor when to do so was physically and mentally consuming. Nameless saints all over the world are putting themselves at risk for the sake of others.

• A saint smiles often.

> *When you come forward as a new norm in a way of sharing the experience rather than acting superior, you trigger the experience in others. If you come forward as superior, others will be offended, or will idolize you, and you will not be able to serve them. Learning how to come forward as a Whole Being, a new model available to all, is the practice you are undertaking.*
>
> —BARBARA MARX HUBBARD,
> *FIFTY-TWO CODES FOR CONSCIOUS EVOLUTION*

18

Can Saints Be Crazy?

We are fools for the sake of Christ, but you are wise in Christ.

—1 Corinthians 4:10

As we set out on the journey this book describes, we trust that we can integrate sanity, spirituality, and sanctity. But sanity and sanctity are not always integrated in the lives of the saints! Jesus was thought of as a madman. St. Joan of Arc, hearing voices, was considered out of her mind. St. Maximilian Kolbe took the place of a prisoner about to be executed—what might be regarded as an insane decision. How ironic that St. Maximilian seems crazy for his behavior in World War II, but war itself is still seen as sane!

Saints are ordinary and joyous people who are often also misfits. Sometimes they look quite crazy or at least foolish. People seems irrational if they were to

- Trust that there really is a higher power than ego
- Love unreservedly, unconditionally, and universally
- Put themselves at risk for others
- Do good to those who hurt them
- Take a life-endangering stand against evil and ignorance
- Jeopardize their freedom for a cause
- Stay in life-threatening situations for the sake of helping others

All these behaviors and beliefs can make others look askance at saints from the past and even saints today. Indeed, the beliefs and actions of saintly people often contradict the dictionary definition of sanity, which is based on continually doing what it takes to survive and thrive within a balanced lifestyle.

Saints do not *choose* to go beyond safe and secure limits. As we noted above, they feel an inescapable drawing power from spiritual forces within. Indeed, these forces call and commandeer them to a love and daring that is, at times, beyond the realm of reason.

Saints or not, we all occasionally act in ways that are outside the range of sanity. Saints may travel to that zone more often but usually with confidence and certainly without regret. We let saintly foolishness be legitimate, admirable, and even humorous. We let playfulness be luminous.

We can also consider what is referred to as "divine madness." This is unusual, often socially unacceptable behavior in persons experiencing religious ecstasy. It can also include highly unconventional, even shocking ideas or actions displayed by people who are involved in spiritually oriented activities. From their perspective, they have found unique realizations about themselves and the divine life. In other words, such inspired people believe they are animated by a revelation to them of the *more* than is commonly known about God. This, in their minds, makes extreme behavior a natural way of expressing their mystical revelations, often apocalyptic. Not all saints engage in divine madness, but it can be part of their teaching or behavior.

Divine madness seems like mental instability to the mainstream population. We see examples of this in extraordinary activities such as speaking in tongues, fainting at healings, or becoming caught up in a spiritual ecstasy. This is not new; it goes back to ancient times. It is, of course, a small minority of the religious or spiritual community that acts in these curious ways.

Pentecostal religions are often associated with such margin-defying behavior. Participants place an emphasis on rapture, a transcendence of the three-dimensional world. Rapture is considered a liberation from the restraints imposed by societal authority and eventually from the planet altogether. Likewise, wild body movements, dancing, flamboyant praying, and prophesying are not thought of as psychotic. Rather, they represent evidence of the presence of a divine Spirit. All these charismatic behaviors are experienced by believers as automatic, not deliberate. The problem, however, is that these extraordinary behaviors often tend to reinforce separateness. As such, they are not about communicating with and linking to others but, rather, declare a specialness that rejects those outside the group. This is madness for less.

In primitive religions, shamans showed signs of mental pathology, but it was accepted as a vehicle for contact with a world beyond this one and for access to healing powers. We might call the shaman's style *madness for more.* From a psychological point of view, a shaman is not psychotic. That diagnosis is applied to people who are out of control and unstable. A shaman knows what he is doing at all times. He enters a trance willingly and comes out of it when he is ready to do so. Another difference is that a psychotic person is bound up in self, but a shaman is fully at the service of the community.

19

The Divine Reversal

Your way of acting must be different from the world's way.

—RULE OF ST. BENEDICT

In the Catholic, Anglican, and Lutheran traditions, January 25 commemorates the conversion of St. Paul to Christianity. On that day last year, I asked myself, *David, do you think you will ever be fully converted to Christ's spiritual path? You have not been committed to the values in the Sermon on the Mount in so many of your choices over the years. You have not fully trusted the power and graces of the Holy Spirit in your life. You do not love with all your might most of the time.* Rather than putting myself down for these inadequacies, I turned each statement of my limitation into a prayer. I can at least say now that I aspire to be converted, and I am dedicating myself to practices that help that happen. I don't expect a full conversion—every action saintly—but, when I hold an enduring intention, I am on the path of practice. That seems satisfactory for now.

The same questions arise in my mind about my Buddhist practice: *Am I committed fully to Buddha's way? Have I found bodhicitta, the commitment to open to the enlightened way and share it with all beings? Do I sit with all that happens in mindfulness? Do I fully commit myself to loving-kindness?* I am turning all these questions into aspirations and daily practices. I am finding the middle path: neither total perfection nor total disregard, just this moment's commitment to goodness in whatever little—or occasionally big—way fits. Indeed, being on the path *is* spiritual progress since conversion is not a once-and-for-all condition like ear-piercing. Conversion is a continuous evolving, like muscle-building. It is a verb, not a noun. Any of us can attune to the sound of that verb.

Christianity or any style of devout dedication has a way of turning everything upside-down. Sanctity is precisely about reversal of the values of the world. Such a reversal of values is the equivalent of *conversion*, which likewise means a turning, a subverting, a reversing. This is not conversion like joining a new religion. It is conversion—committing to what religion is really about, a new set of values, a new worldview, a new relationship with the divine. Everything is happening in a different way from before, a shocking, seemingly foolish way. Saints are converts to the topsy-turvy, to the upside-down, to the upturned overturned.

The Gospels propose this subversive way of living, accessible to all but unappealing to most. It is a style of behavior that subverts societal values. It does not condone violence, focus on profit, exploit the environment, or accept and normalize inequities in society. Instead, in gospel living, we operate out of a new worldview that overturns worldly attitudes, practices, and interests.

Our reversals are evident in all that we are and do: We act with loving-kindness to those who hate us. We do not retaliate in kind. We eschew aggression. We bless those who curse us rather than curse them back. We pray for those who mistreat us rather than cause them equal harm. We take a stand against economic and environmental injustice. This will take focusing on obstacles on our path as if they were challenges, not roadblocks. To do this, we give up caution in favor of boldness—a grace we can ask of the Holy Spirit.

Regarding money, our goal is not to hold onto all our personal wealth while others are hungry. We use our riches to care for ourselves and our families. Yet we also contribute, generously and reasonably, to those who are in need: "All who believed were together and had all things in common; they would sell their possessions and goods and distribute the proceeds to all, as any had need" (Acts 2:44–45). In saintliness, we go one step further and do all we can to change the institutions that support and prolong the injustices. Pope St. Paul VI's encyclical *Populorum Progressio (On the Development of Peoples)* speaks to us today: "The hungry nations of the world cry out to the peoples blessed with abundance. And the Church, cut to the quick by this cry, asks each and every man to hear his brother's plea and answer it lovingly" (no. 3). And as the United States Conference of Catholic Bishops' Department of Justice, Peace, and Human Development noted on the fiftieth anniversary of the encyclical, "We must work towards a world where all people can be 'artisans of their destiny' and where 'the needy Lazarus can sit down with the rich man at the same banquet table.' The economy must be made to serve the human person (instead of the other way around). . . . Inequality is a global issue, and wealthy countries should act to help nations in need through 'aid,' relief for poor countries 'overwhelmed by debt,' 'equitable trade relations,' 'hospitable reception' for immigrants, and, for businesses operating in foreign countries, a focus on 'social progress' instead of 'self-interest.' Sadly, these are all issues still in need of our attention."[3]

The upside-down vision of Jesus did not sit well with some of his contemporaries. They particularly did not like the fact that he refused to damn the Gentiles, and that he did not promise punishment and expulsion of the Romans. For Jesus, holy reversal even took the form of welcoming all to the table, to including those who were supposed to be excluded (see Acts 6:1–6).

In a letter to the Roman governor, Judge Marcellinus, regarding the punishment of those convicted of killing Christians, St. Augustine, a convert to Christianity, wrote, "We do not wish to have the sufferings of the servants of God avenged by the infliction of precisely similar injuries in the way of retaliation. . . . But who does not see that when

---

[3] USCCB Department of Justice, Peace, and Human Development, "Blessed Pope Paul VI's Call for Peace and Justice Challenges Us More Than Ever on 50th Anniversary of Populorum Progressio," To Go Forth (blog), March 23, 2017.

a restraint is put upon the boldness of savage violence, and the remedies fitted to produce repentance are not withdrawn, this discipline should be called a benefit rather than vindictive punishment?"[4] What an admirable example of how true conversion leads to Christ-like reversal in our actions and attitudes!

In our call to be saints, we treat everyone as an equal rather than support or enjoy class distinctions. We do not have prejudices against others because of their differences. We do not exclude others or persecute them on the basis of political views, religious preference, gender or sexual orientation, race, or immigration or economic status. We believe that all people are equal in value and deserve equal respect and equal loving-kindness.

Let's explore the concept of reversal of lifestyle and attitude in the Beatitudes. They are listed in the Sermon on the Mount, the heart of the teaching on divine reversal. Here we can appreciate the kingdom Jesus had in mind for the poor and the rejected, the off-scouring of all. His new world is to be built on a radical rejection of the world of his day, and also the street world that exists today, with its motives of greed, abuse, and division:

> When Jesus saw the crowds, he went up the mountain; and after he sat down, his disciples came to him. Then he began to speak, and taught them, saying:
>
> "Blessed are the poor in spirit, for theirs is the kingdom of heaven.
>
> "Blessed are those who mourn, for they will be comforted.
>
> "Blessed are the meek, for they will inherit the earth.
>
> "Blessed are those who hunger and thirst for righteousness, for they will be filled.
>
> "Blessed are the merciful, for they will receive mercy.

---

[4] St. Augustine, "Letter CXXXIII" (AD 412) to Marcellinus (no. 1), *Augustine Letters* 198.

"Blessed are the pure in heart, for they will see God.

"Blessed are the peacemakers, for they will be called children of God.

"Blessed are those who are persecuted for righteousness' sake, for theirs is the kingdom of heaven.

"Blessed are you when people revile you and persecute you and utter all kinds of evil against you falsely on my account. Rejoice and be glad, for your reward is great in heaven, for in the same way they persecuted the prophets who were before you." (Matt 5:1–12)

The last verse indicates that the style of reversal of the world's way was always part of saintly living. Indeed, we see it in the Old Testament: "For though the Lord is high, he regards the lowly; but the haughty he perceives from far away" (Ps 138:6). Here we also realize that grace is the divine response to our commitment to reversal.

The oppressed groups mentioned in the Beatitudes are not being touted as better off. Indeed, the Sermon on the Mount is being presented by the very person who said he had come to set the captives free. Jesus knows they are the victims of the world of domination, subjugation, and tyranny. The social evils they suffer are certainly not the penalty of a punitive God or a sign of privilege. Jesus has come to set the browbeaten free, the very opposite of what an unjust society thrives on.

Divine reversal has challenging personal implications too. In Jesus's time, looking good in the eyes of others and avoiding embarrassment or shame were two major concerns. If one person harmed another or sullied his reputation, the victim would incur further shame if he did not retaliate as soon as possible, and as fiercely. Aristotle confirms this primitive view in his *Rhetoric*: "To take just revenge on enemies and refuse to be reconciled is praiseworthy; for to retaliate is just." In the ancient world, this is how a person recovered his honor and saved himself from being thought of as a weakling.

The Sermon on the Mount turns all this upside down. Jesus calls shameful what was considered honorable, and honorable what was thought of as shameful. He reverses the meaning of honor and shame, a revolutionary feat. The Sermon on the Mount suggests that committing to this reversal is true holiness. For early Christians, a commitment to reversal became a double blow. Not only did the believer endure the original insult and then not get a chance to avenge it. But his neighbors then further disparaged him for seeming too weak to embrace society's standard of responding to abuse.

Aristotle also recommends refusing to be reconciled with our oppressor. Jesus specifically reverses this suggestion. He tells us to leave our gift at the altar if our brother has something against us. In other words, religious rituals lose their effectiveness when we still act in accord with an honor-focused society. True honor, for Jesus, is granting primacy to reconciliation. This means letting go of the ego's insistence on playing its favorite game: revenge. It is also letting go of the ego's greatest fear: losing face. Saints want to have only Jesus's face, and it wears a crown of thorns. Saints don't care about losing face, only losing Jesus's face.

The Magnificat of Mary, the song she sang when she visited her cousin Elizabeth, lists other striking reversals: "He has brought down the powerful from their thrones, and lifted up the lowly; he has filled the hungry with good things, and sent the rich away empty" (Luke 1:52–53).

The same theme of reversal occurs earlier in Scripture. Hannah, the mother of the prophet Samuel, like Mary, utters a similar Magnificat: "My heart exults in the Lord. . . . I rejoice in my victory. . . . The bows of the mighty are broken, but the feeble gird on strength. Those who were full have hired themselves out for bread, but those who were hungry are fat with spoil. The Lord makes poor and makes rich; he brings low, he also exalts. He raises up the poor from the dust; he lifts the needy from the ash heap, to make them sit with princes and inherit a seat of honor" (1 Sam 2:2–8).

Privilege, wealth, prestige, and power will have their day but will not be the last word. In the "kingdom come," we keep praying that injustice can turn into justice, war into peace, hate into love. Martin Luther King Jr. reminds us that this optimistic option is already happening, albeit slowly: "The arc of the moral universe is long, but it bends toward justice."[5]

Our trust in the Spirit of Christ implies the possibility of achieving a radical reversal of the established order of war, hatred, and avarice in our day and age. We are advised to embrace the divine reversal by St. Paul: "Do not be conformed to this world, but be transformed by the renewing of your minds, so that you may discern what is the will of God—what is good and acceptable and perfect" (Rom 12:2). We can make a heart-move in the direction of a new world order, the "perfect will." It is through the "renewing" that we show the world the bigness of our faith.

A saint appreciates religion for its capacity to help us embrace reversal, a pathway to a living relationship with Christ. A saint is cautious about organized religion since it might not support all this. For instance, a church may uphold the inclination of society toward war by not encouraging conscientious objection in its young members. This collusion between church and state is what a saint seeks to oppose, overturn, and reverse. When religion, however, supports gospel reversal, a saint is in with both jubilant feet.

The most striking reversal in the Christian gospel is sacrifice as depicted in the crucifixion. Jesus chooses shameful suffering and unjust execution as the passport to resurrection for himself and us. This choice of dishonor and shame is called the "scandal of the cross." If we want the life of sanctity, we take up that same cross, its crossbars showing the sign of divine reversal.

The reversal theme is certainly Jesus's teaching. Yet it is also his *promise* as we see in these two Gospel passages: "Indeed, some are last

---

[5] Martin Luther King Jr., "Our God Is Marching On!" March 25, 1965, The Martin Luther King Jr. Research and Education Institute, Stanford University.

who will be first, and some are first who will be last" (Luke 13:30), and "All who exalt themselves will be humbled, and all who humble themselves will be exalted" (Matt 23:12).

> *A swift reversal is making us aware that your [Je-*
> *sus's] main purpose in this revealing to us of your*
> *heart was to enable our love to escape from the con-*
> *strictions of . . . too limited an image of you. . . .*
> *What I discern in your breast is simply a furnace of*
> *fire; and the more I fix my gaze on its ardency the*
> *more it seems to me that all around it the contours*
> *of your body melt away and become enlarged beyond*
> *all measure, till the only features I can distinguish*
> *in you are those of the face of a world which has*
> *burst into flame.*
>
> —Pierre Teilhard de Chardin,
> "The Mass on the World,"
> in *The Heart of Matter*

20

Sanctity Tailored
to Who We Are

In Catholic religious life, some orders are devoted to a life of action
in and for the world. Some are called to a life of contemplation,
praying for the world while remaining cloistered from it. Some orders combine contemplation with an apostolic commitment in the
world. All three options can be appreciated as equal in value. Prayer
for the world is as important as social action in it. We hear Pope
Alexander IV at the canonization of the Franciscan contemplative
St. Clare in 1255:

> O Clare, endowed in a manifold manner with titles of clarity!
> Before thy conversion (thou were) indeed clear, in thy conver-
> sion clearer, in thy comportment in the cloister outstandingly
> clear, and after having run down the space of thy present life
> thou has begun to shine as most clear! This light, indeed,
> remained enclosed in secret cloisters, and outside it emitted
> sparkling rays; it was gathered together in a strict convent, and
> it was sprinkled upon the entire age; it was guarded within, and
> it flowed forth outside. For indeed, Clare lay hidden, but her
> life lay open; Clare was silent, but her fame shouted out; she
> was concealed in her cell and she was known among cities. . . .
> The whole court of the Church has been filled full in every

manner with the odors of her sanctity. From her enclosure she illumined the wide world.[6]

Every description of sanctity listed earlier can be fulfilled also by a contribution of prayer for the world's needs. We can trust that either style is valuable. Both Martha and Mary are saints.

We design our life of practice in accord with our own personality traits, talents, time constraints, and personal limitations. This is how we integrate sanity, spirituality, and sanctity. Regarding religious orders, we see that each has what is called a charism. This is a gift of the Holy Spirit bestowed on individuals or focused faith groups to benefit the entire Church. Technically, charisms refer to extraordinary powers especially active in the early Church. Some were described in chapter 18. Charisms nowadays can also include a prophetic voice, an ability to heal, a sharp intuitive sense, and a contemplative orientation that leads to mystical realizations.

Recently, the meaning of the word "charism" has been expanded. It refers to *how special graces help a focused group fulfill its purpose effectively.* For instance, the Dominicans were founded to preach the gospel. Thus, they can rely on the Holy Spirit for the charism of preaching effectively. The Religious of the Sacred Heart have the charism of spreading the knowledge and love of Christ's heart in the world. They rely not only on their own talents to do this; they have help from the Sacred Heart of Jesus.

From a psychological point of view, each of us was born with an endowment of gifts and talents. Fred Astaire did not learn to dance as he did; he was born with a larger capacity and ease in dancing than most of us have. He practiced dancing but only in response to his inborn talent. In addition, his personality was outgoing enough to

---

[6] The Bull of Pope Alexander IV, "Clara claris praeclara," on the canonization of St. Clare of Assisi, co-foundress of the Poor Clares. Latin text taken from S. Brufani, *Fontes Franciscani,* E. Menestò, S. Brufani, et al., eds. (Assisi: Edizioni Porziuncola, 1995), 2331–37,

become a public performer. Likewise, each of us has unique gifts that, with practice, we can build upon. It may be in sports, art, language, skilled labor, science, acting, child-rearing, political savvy, and so on. Each of us also has innate introverted or extraverted personality characteristics. In the best life plan, we design our work and our relationships in accord with our personality style and the gifts we were given.

As body-mind beings, we all have talents and gifts. As spiritual beings we all have graces. As saintly beings we have one—or many—charisms. We can't help noticing it. Others will see it in us. Our only task is to use it for the good of all beings. We can trust receiving graces to fulfill this purpose.

We came here to be saints. But "saint" is a signature word, different in meaning and expression for each saintly soul. Each of the millions of saints who have lived on our planet have been unique and therefore had singular charisms. All saints ultimately have the same resolve: to be Christ in the world of their lifetime. Each has his or her unique way of showing it.

We can trust that when we are focused on being Christ in our own unique way, the Spirit of Christ is animating and blessing our purpose with a charism tailored to our natural gifts. Each of us can ask: *what is the charism I seek in my own life, in my world, here and now?* We find it sometimes by noticing whom we admire. We usually admire in others what is hidden in us, waiting to be expressed. We strongly respect in saints those qualities that we may have disavowed or been too self-doubting or unwilling to allow to shine in ourselves. We have not dared to believe in our inherent holy wholeness. The Dalai Lama's charism for nonviolence, Mother St. Teresa's charism for caring for the poor, Dorothy Day's charism for work toward societal change, Grandma's charism for a life of sacrifice for her family—all await our imitation in our own life now.

We can usually find our charism at the meeting of talent and opportunity. We were blessed with a talent for getting things done and we have a chance to work or volunteer in a program for societal change.

We might also find our charism at the meeting of resource and need. For instance, with generous hearts, we can contribute to a local program that helps migrants or takes a stand against racism, anti-gay hate crimes, or human trafficking.

We can trust that something is afoot in the universe that wants to connect all the gifts we have with all the needs others have. There is no duplicate of ourselves before, during, or after our lifetime, so our part in such a purpose is not only unique but necessary if all that we are is to get its chance to bloom.

> *I say yes to everything that happens to me today as an opportunity to give and receive love and to free myself from fear.*
>
> *I am grateful for the enduring capacity to love that has come to me from the Sacred Heart of the universe.*
>
> *May everything that happens to me today open my heart more.*
>
> *May all that I think, say, feel, do, and am express loving-kindness toward myself, those close to me, and all beings.*
>
> *May love be my life purpose, my bliss, my destiny, my calling, and the richest grace I can receive or give.*
>
> *May I always be especially compassionate toward people who are considered least or last, or who feel alone or lost.*

21

Companions Here and Hereafter

> *We can choose to be guardian angels who protect,*
> *care for, and transform the earth into a common*
> *home for all, the entire earthly and cosmic com-*
> *munity.*
>
> —MARK HATHAWAY AND LEONARDO BOFF,
> *THE TAO OF LIBERATION*

For Christians, sanctity is founded on friendship with Christ. It is like companionship with one who loves all of us unconditionally and a call to do likewise. To have faith is to trust that there is a guiding or protecting presence with us. Jesus calls himself our good shepherd and expands the "Thou art with me" of the Twenty-third Psalm to a promise of companionship on and off planet: "And remember, I am with you always" (Matt 28:20).

As we have already noted, we have access to three resources. For example, if we are fearful and open to being helped, our psychological resource is companionship with a therapist or self-help practice; our spiritual resource is companionship with a spiritual director, mentor, or guide. Our holy companions are Christ and the communion of saints, including people we respect as saints in our lives today. Communion means that we are in this together, all helping one another. We call on saints to help us relinquish fear. We assist those who fear as we do.

The impulse to ask for help from powers beyond us is found in all religions. In the Judeo-Christian tradition, this can be seen in our belief in guardian angels. We see the same guarding energy personified in ancient Greece in Hermes, guide of souls. In Japanese Buddhism, Jizo Bodhisattva guides and accompanies travelers and watches over children especially. The Japanese Buddhist teacher Dogen Zenji wrote, "Arousing the aspiration for awakening is making a vow to free all sentient beings from suffering before freeing oneself, and actualizing the vow. . . . This aspiration arises in the mystical *communion between Buddhas and sentient beings.*"[7]

We can compare statements about this communion from various traditions. In ancient times, Plutarch noted, "According to Hesiod, the souls delivered from birth are at rest and absolved. They become guardian spirits of humankind. . . . Like old athletes, they do not lose interest in us but show goodwill and sympathetic zeal to us still engaged in life, setting forth with us and shouting encouragement as they see us approach, and at last attain, our hoped-for goal" (*De Genio Socratis* 24).

In the Catholic tradition, St. Thérèse wrote in her autobiography, "I want to spend my heaven doing good on earth."[8] She did not want heaven as a personal reward, only as a venue to continue her work, to "shower roses" of grace on our spiritually parched planet. St. Thérèse also saw how a place in the communion of saints awaited her just for this.

Again, in the Catholic tradition, we hear from Pierre Teilhard de Chardin in *Hymn of the Universe*, "One by one—more vaguely it is true, yet all-inclusively—I call before me the whole vast anonymous army of living humanity; those who surround me and support me though I do not know them; those who come, and those who go; above all, those who in office, laboratory and factory, through their vision of truth or despite their error, truly believe in the progress of

---

[7] Edited from a talk by Kokyo Henkel, "Mystical Communion," *Sangha* (January 2015).

[8] St. Thérèse of Lisieux, *Story of a Soul* (Washington, DC: ICS Publications, 1975), 211.

earthly reality and who today will take up again their impassioned pursuit of the light."[9]

Regarding the communion of saints in the Protestant tradition, Dag Hammarskjöld wrote in *Markings*, "Through me there flashes this vision of a magnetic field in the soul, created in a timeless present by unknown multitudes, living in holy obedience, whose words and actions are a timeless prayer. —'The Communion of Saints'—and—within it—an eternal life."[10]

This mention of "eternal life" awakens our interest and makes us perhaps wonder about how to configure the idea of heaven in our day: From a psychological perspective we find a comment on peak experiences from Abraham Maslow: "The conception of heaven that emerges from the peak experiences is one which exists all the time all around us."[11]

Pope St. John Paul echoed this same idea: "We know that the 'heaven' or 'happiness' in which we will find ourselves is neither an abstraction nor a physical place in the clouds, but a living, personal relationship with the Holy Trinity. It is our meeting with the Father which takes place in the risen Christ through the communion of the Holy Spirit."[12]

In our secular world, these statements may seem quaint and anachronistic. They may even seem like wishful thinking. If they strike a chord in us personally or reflect our experience, however, we will surely cherish them. We can find comfort likewise in Martin Luther King Jr.'s statement that we are not alone in our saintly endeavors. We can trust in a "cosmic companionship" always around us. And, of

---

[9] Pierre Teilhard de Chardin, *Hymn of the Universe* (New York, Harper & Row, 1961), 18.

[10] Dag Hammarskjöld, *Markings* (1964; New York: Ballantine, 1983), 71.

[11] Abraham H. Maslow, *Religions, Values, and Peak Experiences* (New York: Penguin Books, 1976), 66.

[12] John Paul II, General Audience, July 21, 1999, no. 4,

course, we ourselves, in saintly longing, might look forward to becoming companions of fellow earthlings when we pass over.

> *I do not want to be saved without you.*
>
> —St. Augustine to his congregation;
> *Sermon* 17.7

> *Please do not build a stupa [tomb] for me. . . . If you must build one, though, please make sure that you put a sign on it that says, "I am not in here." In addition, you can also put another sign that says, "I am not out there either," and a third sign that says, "If I am anywhere, it is in your mindful breathing and in your peaceful steps."*
>
> —Thich Nhat Hanh,
> interview with Brother Phap Dung, 2019

22

Universal Love

Here I understand what they call glory: the right to
love without limit.

—Epitaph of Albert Camus

A universal love is possible in anyone who is sane, spiritually aware, saintly, or none of the above. It can take the form of interpersonal love and intimacy that extends beyond a relationship into the world. It can be social and take the form of contributing to causes that benefit the oppressed. It can mean joining a peace corps. It can show itself in caring compassion for a needy humanity or be as simple as offering a universal intention when doing small, ordinary acts. For instance, when filling a water pitcher we might inwardly affirm, "May all humans have pure and plentiful water."

In spiritual consciousness we appreciate the striking wisdom in a statement from the Jewish-Roman historian Flavius Josephus in *Contra Apionem:* "I suppose it will become evident that the laws in the Torah are meant to lead to a universal love of humanity." Indeed, we can see all our spiritual practices as pathways to a universal caring connection. Every Mass, every rosary, every novena, and every candle we light all have one purpose: to make us love more. This is the essential more of the saintly life.

In the Buddhist tradition, we take a bodhisattva vow "to save all beings." A bodhisattva is an enlightened person who does not seek to enter nirvana until he can bring all beings with him into enlightenment.

He offers unreserved compassion to all beings. The bodhisattva path equates compassion and nirvana. This is a profound insight into the religious term "salvation." As we noted above, when St. Thérèse says she will spend her heaven doing good on earth, she is saying that love *is* salvation. No matter what, loving is heaven on earth, the land of milk and honey, in our own neighborhood.

Compassion is love as an empathic response to suffering. In some spiritual traditions, suffering is to be embraced as salutary, redemptive. In psychological health, we don't seek pain. We find a path through it into personal growth. Suffering, then, helps us open to others. We might do this in two ways: We feel compassion for others when they suffer, and we seek support from them when we suffer. These are two of the many ways to find value in suffering.

In our practice of love and compassion, we do not demand perfection of ourselves. That would be a denial of the role of grace in our work. We simply do our best. Fred Rogers (a.k.a. "Mister Rogers") said this in his acceptance speech when Mr. Rogers' Neighborhood won the 2001 Special Christopher Award:

> I have recognized that the space between a person who is doing his or her best and a person who has come in need, that space is holy ground. The Holy Spirit can use whatever we offer to speak to another person's heart. So whenever I make a television program or give a speech or just talk with a neighbor, I realize that all I need to do is give the best that I can, and God will translate it into whatever is needed most.[13]

One does not need religion to arrive at this level of social caring. We have seen it in unchurched people whom we have known and admired over the years. The ancient pagan atheistic writer Lucretius,

---

[13] Tony Rossi, "Mr. Rogers on Judgment, Need, and Holy Ground," Patheos. com, May 13, 2013.

for example, declares the spiritual wisdom that the birth of one thing is always the death of another. Declaring that the world is eternally new and that all mortal beings live by mutual interchange, he compares them to runners in a relay race handing on the torch of life.[14] From this perspective, we are committed to ethical behavior because it honors our connection with all our fellow humans.

Creative concrete actions, however small, are our personal response to the harsh given of our human inclination toward evil. We believe "the end of the world" means the end of this kind of a world. We presume that end may not happen once and for all. But we believe it does happen in any moment when we make a choice for love over hate.

> *May I show all the love I have*
> *In any way I can, wherever I may be,*
> *Today and all the time,*
> *To everyone—including me—*
> *Since love is what we are*
> *And why we're here.*
> *Now nothing matters to me more*
> *Or gives me greater joy.*
> *May all our world become*
> *One Sacred Heart of love.*

---

[14] Lucretius, *On the Nature of Things,* trans. Martin Ferguson Smith (Indianapolis: Hackett, 2001), book II, ll. 76–78.

23

Opening
to the Holy Spirit

You will receive the gift of the Holy Spirit.

—Acts 2:38

When we realize that there is no separate, distant, dualistic God, the divine life becomes not an entity but a life force both within and around us. There is still a God presence, just not with the same duties to perform for us. Instead, our life becomes a collaborative work with a communion of saints, and devotion is enlivened by a combination of our work and the grace of the Holy Spirit of love, wisdom, and healing. This life-giving Spirit is our deepest identity as sane, spiritual, and saintly humans. Theologian Jürgen Moltmann wrote, "We continually experience the Holy Spirit as both a divine counterpart to whom we call, and a divine presence in which we call—as the space we live in."[15]

Pope Francis, in his Morning Meditation on April 16, 2013, echoing these words, said, "Surrender to the Holy Spirit, to that Spirit *who comes from within us* and makes us go forward on the path of holiness." We hear this same teaching from St. Basil in "On the Holy Spirit":

---

[15] Jürgen Moltmann, *The Source of Life: The Holy Spirit and the Theology of Life,* trans. Margaret Kohl (Minneapolis: Augsburg Fortress, 1997), 11.

"Through the Spirit we acquire a likeness to God; indeed, we attain what is beyond our most sublime aspirations—we become God."[16]

Meditation and Reflection

Saints have an ongoing devotion to the Holy Spirit, both as God within and God everywhere. The following quotations show how the Holy Spirit can become a real presence in our lives. Read them and the brief comment that follows each one meditatively and ask the indwelling Spirit to come alive in your own life.

God's love has been poured into our hearts through the Holy Spirit that has been given to us. (Rom 5:5)

God's love is the Holy Spirit. This is the love in us and in the immensities of the universe without limit or end. Only a God-within could be a love like that. When we are open to the grace of this love, our love, the indwelling Spirit shows itself unconditionally and universally. This grace is always and already ours. Every moment is an opportunity for this love to open in us and through us. (This is why there are moments!)

Our inadequacies cannot contravene our capacity to love. We hear from Pope Francis in his encyclical *Laudato Si'*: "For all our limitations, gestures of generosity, solidarity, and caring cannot but well up within us, since we are made for love" (no. 58). Events, no matter how disastrous, cannot cancel the power of divine love in us. All that we do or are, all that others do or are, all that happens to us, all that befalls us in the world around us—all are vehicles by which the Holy Spirit shows her love through us. To take advantage of these opportunities is

---

[16] St. Basil the Great, "On the Holy Spirit," chs. 9, 22–23. It is used in the Roman Liturgy's Office of Readings during the days between the Feast of the Ascension and the Feast of Pentecost, on Tuesday of the seventh week of Easter.

why we are who we are, why others are as they are, why things happen to us, why anything occurs. Nothing is about anything but love.

> The Spirit helps us in our weakness; for we do not know how
> to pray as we ought, but that very Spirit intercedes with sighs
> too deep for words. (Rom 8:26)

The Holy Spirit, helping us "in our weakness," is an empowering
force, giving us the courage to stand up to injustice, to love and care
for all beings, to co-create a planet that is safe from predation. The
Holy Spirit is likewise our personal Advocate and the world's too, as
we pursue the saintly path. This is also the Spirit of divine love, wisdom, and healing—three qualities of God that by grace are resources
in our higher self. When we say, "God is love," we mean the Holy
Spirit is our own identity. When we say the Holy Spirit is a source
of healing and reconciliation to humankind, we are describing our
own vocation. In the *Phaedrus*, Plato describes "the colorless, formless,
intangible essence." He characterizes it as "divine intelligence," "pure
knowledge," "truth," "reality," "absolute knowledge." Experiencing this
inner field, one "is replenished and made glad."[17] We can ask the Spirit
to make that our experience too.

> The Spirit is always speaking to us deep in our hearts, if only
> we listen. . . . If I had my life to live over again, I would live it
> in complete openness to the Holy Spirit. (St. Madeleine Sophie
> Barat, 1779–1865)

St. Madeleine Sophie considered the Holy Spirit to be the true
founder of her order, the Religious of the Sacred Heart. In her statement she shows us that the Holy Spirit is never mute, always speaking
to us, encouraging us toward wholeness and holiness. We look back

---

[17] Plato, *Phaedrus*, trans. Benjamin Jowett (Bulgaria: Demetra Publishing, 2019).

over our life decisions. We wonder how different our life would be if each had been aligned with the counsel of the Holy Spirit. We would then have prayed each day, "Holy Spirit, show me what you want of me and give me the grace to do and be it." But, even as of today, it is not too late. We can bring the Holy Spirit of love into our present and future choices. We can be self-caring and live in caring connection. We do this by contemplation with an apostolic intent. We pray *and* act. The Holy Spirit is the bridge of grace between those two.

> Pressure [to evolve] is what we have always called the Holy Spirit. (Judy Cannato, *Field of Compassion*)

"Self-transcendence" refers to the *more* that characterizes all of spirituality. That *more* is the Holy Spirit at work in us as an impulse of evolution: the Spirit propels us to move beyond our limits into a wider sense of ourselves and our purpose. We become open to new vistas of what life and politics can be about, a world of freedom, non-violence, and mutuality. We begin to see both the light and dark sides of ourselves and others. We look for ways to befriend the shadow side in ourselves and bring healing to it so that its creative energies can move in the direction of goodness. Everything in us is poised to take this direction. There is one who waits in us with sacred expectancy, the Holy Spirit of oneness.

> To continue to place our hopes in a social order achieved by external violence would simply amount to our giving up all hope of carrying the Spirit of the Earth to its limits. (Teilhard de Chardin, *Building the Earth*)

The Christian revolution happens under the banner of the Spirit of love. Only saints can be revolutionary in the gospel sense, equality and mercy as our watchwords. The Holy Spirit hears the cries of the dispossessed, the oppressed, the hungry, the homeless, the disappeared, and the lost. Our move toward sanctity is to let the Holy Spirit hear the cries of the world in our hearts and ears. We do not simply listen since the Spirit is summoning us to take some kind of action against injustice, even if it can only be a donation or a letter to a congressperson. The Holy Spirit may come to us as a visceral feeling also. For instance, we might feel moved at a bodily level at the plight of the war-torn. That is an invitation to action. *In spiritual consciousness, what touches us calls us.*

Meditation and Action

Here are ten quotations on this theme. They can be launching pads from meditation to action. I have arranged them so that each one builds on the next. Our goal is exuberant holiness (the only kind):

We hear the call in the daily psychological issues we face. We hear the call in the givens of life, the conditions of our existence. We ask for the grace to be ready for what comes.

As servants of God we have commended ourselves in every way: through great endurance, in afflictions, hardships, calamities, beatings, imprisonments, riots, labors, sleepless nights, hunger; by purity, knowledge, patience, kindness, holiness of spirit, genuine love, truthful speech, and the power of God; with the weapons of righteousness for the right hand and for the left; in honor and dishonor, in ill repute and good repute. We are treated as impostors, and yet are true; as unknown, and yet are well known; as dying, and see—we are alive; as punished, and yet not killed; as sorrowful, yet always rejoicing; as poor, yet making many rich; as having nothing, and yet possessing everything. (2 Cor 6:4–10)

There is nothing so bad, no part of us so wounded that is not redeemable by Christ's love. This is what is really meant by "taking Christ as our redeemer."

Everything that is hurt,
Everything that seemed to us dark, harsh, shameful,
Maimed, ugly, irreparably damaged,
Is in Christ transformed
And recognized as whole, as lovely,
As radiant in Light. (St. Simeon the New Theolo-
   gian, *Hymns of Divine Love 15*)

Our Christ-likeness is complete when we respond to the person in need right here in front of us. The Good Samaritan is the model for Christian charity. Love extends to all beings through service to this very one.

Since you cannot show goodness to everyone, you are to focus your special attention on those who cross your path by coincidence of time, place, or circumstance . . . as though by a sort of lot. (St. Augustine, "On Christian Doctrine")

Every subtle form of elitism—racist, political, or otherwise—is contrary to the call of Christ to love others as he loved us.

We who hated and killed one another and would not share our lives with certain people because of their ethnic differences from us now live intimately with them. (Justin Martyr, *First Apology 14*)

We can't always rely on our own church community for support in engaging in social action. We look for the community that stands for peace and justice, regardless of whether it is the one we were born into.

We also know that religion, as the Marxists have always insisted, has, too often, like an opiate, tended to put people to sleep to the reality and the need for the present struggle for peace and justice. (Dorothy Day, *Catholic Worker*, November 1959)

Christ said he came for the poor—in body, mind, spirit. This primacy is meant to be our primary concern too. There is no meeting Jesus except through our becoming resources to those in need.

The mystery of the poor is this: That they are Jesus, and what you do for them you do for Him. It is the only way we have of knowing and believing in our love. The mystery of poverty is that by sharing in it, making ourselves poor in giving to others, we increase our knowledge of and belief in love. (Dorothy Day, *Catholic Worker*, April 1964)

Poverty, hunger, and deprivation are not acceptable facts of life. They are the consequences of economic injustice. We are Christ on earth today when we look carefully at what we support in our society and ask how it may be part of the system that keeps others oppressed.

The poor person does not exist as an inescapable fact of destiny. His or her existence is not politically neutral, and it is not ethically innocent. The poor are a by-product of the system in which we live and for which we are responsible. They are marginalized by our social and cultural world. They are the oppressed, exploited proletariat, robbed of the fruit of their labor and despoiled of their humanity. Hence the poverty of the poor is not a call to generous relief action, but a demand that we go and build a different social order. (Gustavo Gutierrez, *A Theology of Liberation*)

Our only chance to survive is in what Thich Nhat Hanh called "interbeing." This is the challenge facing us now as a nation and as individuals. As Teilhard says, this means standing against divisiveness of all kinds since that is what leads to war and aggression.

The Age of Nations is past. The task before us now, if we would not perish, is to build the Earth. . . . We have reached a crossroads in human evolution where the only road which leads forward is towards a common passion. (Teilhard de Chardin, *Building the Earth*)

This next quotation follows on and goes into the specific challenges we might encounter. We see how to move from an essential ongoing heart-commitment to daily existential choices that make our commitment concrete.

We cherish this hope: that distrust and selfishness among nations will eventually be overcome by a stronger desire for mutual collaboration and a heightened sense of solidarity. We hope that the developing nations will take advantage of their geographical proximity to one another to organize on a broader territorial base and to pool their efforts for the development of a given region. We hope that they will draw up joint programs, coordinate investment funds wisely, divide production quotas fairly, and exercise management over the marketing of these products. We also hope that multilateral and broad international associations will undertake the necessary work of organization to find ways of helping needy nations, so that these nations may escape from the fetters now binding them; so that they themselves may discover the road to cultural and social progress, while remaining faithful to the native genius of their land. (Pope Paul VI, *On the Development of Peoples*, no. 64)

Finally, we consider how we might take a stand individually, animated by conscience, but always in accord with our individual gifts and limits. For John Dear the stand is a path to prison. For us it has to be the calling we hear, yet with no holding back, no forcing. Only the Holy Spirit can show us that personal choice.

It's a powerful experience to stand before a judge and be sentenced to jail for saying No to war, injustice and nuclear weapons, something I highly recommend for all followers of the nonviolent Jesus. It really helps clarify one's discipleship, one's citizenship in God's reign of peace, one's faith, hope and love. In these days of war, genocide, nuclear weapons, poverty, executions, abortion, torture, global warming, and violence of every description, it's a great grace to be in trouble with the empire for practicing nonviolence, for daring to offer a word of peace, for serving the God of peace.

—JOHN DEAR,
STATEMENT IN COURT, 2007

24

Practicing Contemplation

Through contemplation, transform your entire being into the image of the Divine One.
—St. Clare, "Letter to Blessed Agnes"

Contemplation is a style of prayer in the mystical tradition of most religions. Thomas Merton, in *Contemplative Prayer*, gives us a clear definition: "Contemplation is essentially a listening in silence, an expectancy. . . . Only when we are able to 'let go' of everything within us, all desire to see, to know, to taste, and to experience the presence of God, do we truly become able to experience that presence with the overwhelming conviction and reality that revolutionize our entire inner life."[18]

Contemplation is not only for saints. It is for all of us, since we can all listen at deep levels. We can distinguish two kinds of listening: ordinary listening and contemplative listening.

With ordinary listening, we hear what is said by concentrating mainly on *content*. We listen to comprehend. We might analyze or evaluate that content as we listen. We listen with our mind. We are persons listening to persons communicating. This is listening as in, "Listen up."

Contemplative listening, however, is receptive. Our focus is on the *process* that happens in us. In receptive listening, we are simply open to

---

[18] Thomas Merton, *Contemplative Prayer* (New York: Image, 1971), 68.

what comes through to us without judgment or censorship, without even a need to reply. We listen mainly with our heart. We tune in to divine cadences. We become a listening presence to a communicative presence. This is listening as in, "Listen in."

To use an analogy, we might say that in ordinary listening, we enter the garden of the other and notice which flowers are in it—their names, their placement, and their colors. In receptive listening, we find ourselves present in a garden simply sitting and feeling the sense of the place.

Here is another example: We listen to a news broadcast and, while listening, we are responding internally with thoughts, including criticisms, worries, projections, protests, and agreement. This is ordinary active listening. When we are at the beach alone listening to the sounds of the ocean waves with no thoughts, we are engaging in receptive listening. We heard the news; we contemplated the waves.

In the quotation at the opening of this chapter, Thomas Merton also noted that in contemplation, we listen with "expectancy." This element of listening reminds us of the early Quaker phrase "waiting worship." The congregants sit in silence waiting for the Holy Spirit to move them, to communicate to them. Likewise, in contemplation, we are cocking an expectant ear to whatever message or call may come to us.

Even if all we receive is a deeper silence, we have heard what we needed to hear. Then contemplative listening is opening in silence to silence. And that silence is enough. As Richard Rohr notes, "Prayer is sitting in the silence until it silences us."[19]

Contemplative prayer is considered both a gift of grace, something that happens in us, and a practice we accomplish with effort. Is there a way to learn from this religious perspective and to be open to this grace/practice? It takes a freedom from dualism, no longer thinking of prayer as a form of communication in which we contact a Being

---

[19] Richard Rohr, *Just This: Prompts and Practices for Contemplation* (London: SPCK, 2018).

in the sky. Contemplation takes us to a new concept of prayer; it is oneness with a *presence within and all around us.* We can think of this presence as the indwelling Spirit, our higher self, our Buddha nature, our deep inner life, a higher power than ego, a field of wholeness. We are not praying to someone for something. But we are learning from the contemplative style of prayer that we can turn to a deeper life in us, something more than we notice in daily life. We open to the essential inner resource, our enlightened nature, always here, always now.

How does contemplation differ from mindfulness? In mindfulness, we let go of thoughts and return to our breath. In contemplation, we let go of thoughts in order to penetrate our deepest reality beyond ego. Both mindfulness and contemplation are essential in our spiritual life. Mindfulness is a form of letting go because it releases us from our attachment to thoughts and judgments. Contemplation takes us further—into the "more." In inner silence, we are finding our own pristine original presence. In mindfulness, we notice and let go. In contemplation, we listen and enter our enlightened nature, never mute for long. This takes dropping any attachment to reaching for a spiritual goal. Then, paradoxically, we experience a presence within that awakens us and opens us to a whole new sense of ourselves and reality, now all one.

Indeed, in mindfulness, *we are pointing* our consciousness in a direction *and* avoiding reflecting on anything in particular. In mystical contemplation, we are being *pointed to* something—or Someone—that takes us to and then beyond reflecting. Likewise, an awareness of the here and now in mindfulness, from the mystical perspective, is not our goal. We are out for higher stakes: an awareness of Buddha, God, higher self *as* the here and now, as we.

We can also explore the practice of contemplation with a look at what the Spanish mystic St. Teresa of Ávila says about contemplative prayer. In *The Way of Perfection* she outlines three phases of it. Each phase builds on the one before; each is a practice. First is the "Prayer of Recollection," in which we submerge our thoughts and feelings in silence and stillness. We keep releasing ourselves from the mind's chatter and then notice openings through which the divine can enter. In the second phase, the "Prayer of Quiet," we are simply staying in and gradually softening into God's tender embrace. We are letting the light and lightness of divine life into our souls. We feel the grace of serenity. We cannot make this happen, but we can be open to it. Finally comes the "Prayer of Oneness" or union. Our individual ego is no longer in charge. All duality has collapsed into unity. Thoughts learn to wait their turn.

Both sanctity and spirituality can include a mystical consciousness—a nondual sense of the divine. Anyone pursuing a spiritual path can move toward mystical contemplation. It is not reserved to religiously oriented people. For instance, a sense of reverence in nature is mystical whether someone believes in God or not.

Mystics from all traditions unanimously recommend certain specific practices: silence, stillness, staying, softening, and solitude. These five S's help us cultivate a mystical spirituality and can ferry us directly into contemplation.

Silence is the realm beyond words and concepts. Words from us to someone denote a duality. Psychologically, we contact feelings beyond separate words. We hear in the poem "Silence," by Marianne Moore, "The deepest feeling always shows itself in silence." Spiritually, it is not we who are silent; it is our deep enlightened presence that is the silence in us.

Silence does not have to mean no sounds. Right now, I hear a crow cawing outside my window and I am letting the sound go as I focus on my writing. Despite the crow's caw, therefore, this is a moment of spiritual silence, not no sounds, but rather not attaching to sounds. When we let the sounds of nature enfold us without grasping or rejecting any one of them—what we learn in mindfulness—the mystery of silence—contemplation—unfolds from within us. We recall Dag Hammarskjöld in his Presidential Address to the Annual Meeting of the Swedish Academy, 1957: "Here man is no longer the center of the world, only a witness, but a witness who is also a partner in the silent life of nature, bound by secret affinities to the trees."[20]

Our mind in constant prattle makes us think that we are never silent, but there is a deep, wordless openness at the base of our being. That is the mystery of our interior silence, a letting go of noisy foreground in favor of the background of divine quietude always in us. In silence our body-mind is not scattered around in thoughts or activities. We are all in one place. Only in our exterior life do we feel separateness. In our interior life there is only oneness.

Stillness refers to inner peace more than to immobility. In fact, we can be still while moving, as T. S. Eliot writes prayerfully to the divine feminine: "We must be still and still moving."[21] Stillness is an interiority so profound that we touch the calm depths within ourselves. No anxiety or movement can interfere or interrupt. We have dropped into a mystical tranquility. We have no place to land permanently, yet we feel fully grounded in reality, another description of real presence. This interior presence is what is meant by "God within." The stillness within is inner peace, another name for resting at last in our human-divine entirety.

Staying is remaining present simply and totally in the here and now without giving in to distractions. We stay put to hear the voice of a deep life in us. We stay put to respond to its call. Our ability to stay and listen is also a grace and a practice. In staying attentively present, we feel the presence of the higher self than ego. In the poem "Stopping by Woods on a Snowy Evening," Robert Frost shows us the power of the contemplative pause in the phrase "stopping here." The "here" is the "here and now" where we take a break from the "promises" we

---

[20] Dag Hammarskjöld, from Presidential Address to the Annual Meeting of the Swedish Academy, "The Linnaeus Tradition and Our Time," December 20, 1957, collected in *Servant of Peace: A Selection of the Speeches and Statements of Dag Hammarskjöld, Secretary-General of the United Nations, 1953–1961* (New York: Harper and Row, 1962), 153.

[21] T. S. Eliot, "East Coker," in *Four Quartets* (Indianapolis: Mariner Books, 1968).

feel obliged to keep in our hubbub world. The same here and now is the divine presence. The sacred pause is adoration of the sacred.

Softening is letting go of demand and control. We are letting go of the need to have something happen. We are becoming receptive to what may come through to us. We are permeable to a power that wants to hold us, either without a ping or with a thud. This is a radical yes to whatever is presenting itself to us in the moment. We will feel the yes *bodily*. It will be making us lighter and opening us to the light. Virginia Woolf writes in *The Waves*, "Month by month, things are losing their hardness; even my body now lets the light through."[22] This is what is meant by softening.

Solitude seems to be the best circumstance for contemplation. We need time alone for the opening that such deep listening makes possible. Solitude is not isolation; it is deep connectedness with all beings. We seem to be alone, but we feel connected more deeply than we do in the presence of others. That is the central paradox of contemplation. We vanish into oneness with no sense of restlessness or loneliness. This is what St. Teresa calls the "Prayer of Oneness" or "Union." We are letting go of any sense of ourselves as separate. What is left of us is our true essential self-in-oneness. This experience is usually brief but memorable and with lasting effects. Our life then changes, and we are no longer so ego-driven, no longer so triggered by what happens to us. We do not make as big a deal of people's negative reactions to us as we once did. With this resilience, our anxiety reduces exponentially. We are wiser and more compassionate. Going in has brought us out.

We cannot make contemplation happen by effort, but these five S's place us in a most apt position for it to occur. They are paths of nonresistance because in each there is no escape, no place to hide, no way of reasoning ourselves into or out of anything, and indeed, no need to know anything at all. We recall the words of the mystic St.

---

[22] Virginia Woolf, *The Waves* (New York: Oxford University Press, 2015), 26.

John of the Cross: "I entered I knew not where and there I stood not knowing, nothing left to know."

In the experience of most mystics, the contemplative sense of oneness with all beings brings a call to service. A *sharing and caring intent* arises from authentic contemplation. We are passionate about committing ourselves to living in accord with the gospel, of spreading it, of acting with the loving-kindness it recommends. We want to share with others the fruits of our contemplative experience. How we do this is unique to each of us. Some of us may show our sharing and caring intent by engaging in social action. Others may do so by contemplative practices, affirmations, prayers for a just world. The particular style of showing our intent is not what matters. What matters is that all that we are and do is dedicated to the welfare of the world—the Jesus vow.

The commitment-to-share element of contemplation presents one of its main purposes. It is not about being all alone at a shrine, having God all to ourselves. It is an activating force that brings us closer to our fellow humans and the world. It is not about finding a path to Christ out there; it is finding and sharing all in him and all of him in all that happens.

In fact, in mystical awareness, we realize that *we* are not contemplating but joining Jesus Christ in his eternal contemplation. We see now what Christ consciousness refers to. Our self-awareness folds into an ongoing liturgy of oneness concelebrated by all of nature and all humanity. This is a dedication to co-create a world of justice, peace, and love—the results of a lifelong program of nonviolence. Such a dedication is a conversion to the purposes of the Sacred Heart of Jesus.

The experience of contemplation does not mean having no distractions or "doing" all five S's successfully. It requires maintaining our pure intention to contemplate and join it to a growing commitment to service. What matters is not giving up the practices and actions that enable that to happen. The purity of our intention and our dedication to practicing *is* success on the contemplative path.

Fully mindful presence in the reality of this moment is direct contact and access to our inner sanctity: limitless love, wisdom, and healing flowing through us into the world. It is happening now and endures for a lifetime. We recall in the words of the poem "Tintern Abbey," by William Wordsworth:

> In this moment there is life and food
> For future years.

We are mindfully remaining in the here and now while letting go of projections, expectations, definitions, and judgments—and any other ego distractions. That letting go fosters the "Prayer of Recollection" and the "Prayer of Quiet." Finally, awareness of our oneness can lead to the compassion and sense of human interrelatedness that come with the "Prayer of Union." Then we hear the voice of God in the neglected cries of the world. Contemplation is how we ready ourselves to hear those cries as a call to silent prayer or to prayer as action.

With a trinitarian awareness we can affirm:

> *May love be how God stays present in my life,*
> *the Sacred Heart of me and all of us,*
> *the Holy Spirit of this whole universe.*

25

Ten Steps to Sanctity
in Our Modern World

The following ten steps reflect and summarize the qualities of sanctity as discussed in this part. Our qualities lead us to take steps. We can then trust that shifts shall happen by grace and we move from "more" to "most."

1. *Surrendering to the divine will.* We can continually free ourselves from self-centeredness. We are then surrendering our will and our lives to a higher power than ego. We are certain that what is happening is exactly what needs to happen so that we can find ourselves in God. Our spiritual practice of unconditional yes to the givens of life has led us to trust them as ingredients of wholeness and holiness. We see the realities we face today as the ways God shows us the next steps on our journey.

Jean-Pierre de Caussade, S.J., wrote in *The Sacrament of the Present Moment,* "The present moment is like an ambassador announcing the policy of God; the heart declares, 'Thy will be done,' and souls, travelling at full speed, never stopping, spread the news far and wide. For them everything without exception is an instrument and means of sanctification, provided that the present moment is all that matters."[23] God's will, as we noted earlier, is nothing less than the reality of what is, what is happening, our predicament in this present moment. We keep saying yes, the surrender that leads to sanctity. Indeed, when we

---

[23] Jean-Pierre de Caussade, S.J., *The Sacrament of the Present Moment,* trans. Kitty Muggeridge (New York: Harper Collins, 1989), 77.

confront reality, with no dodging or damming, we are saying, "Thy will be done." St. Teresa of Ávila summarizes and integrates sanctity with sanity and spirituality in this often attributed saying: "When we accept what happens to us and make the best of it, we are praising God." This is not a promise that all will turn out for the best but we will always have an opportunity to make the best of how things turn out. Then all is praise and gratitude.

2. *Praying always.* We pray always, that is, we are continually listening to the voice of the Holy Spirit as she prays in us. We seek, through prayer and meditation, a more personal relationship with Christ. In other words, our only search is for what is searching for us. We pray to become saints, people who love God, a parenting power, a redeeming power, a loving power. We trust that we were given a lifetime, in vessels of clay, for this almighty love to show itself dazzlingly in us. We engage in contemplation often or daily as described earlier.

3. *Trusting grace.* We trust that God supports our efforts. We trust the power of grace, our holy assisting force, as we focus on our three life goals of sanity, spirituality, and sanctity. We are assured of a grace-presence, a reliable companionship that feels personal and helps us make it through no matter how lonely or woebegone we may feel. If everything we wanted has failed to happen, if every hope has been dashed, we still have the assurance that we will, nonetheless, be able somehow to "walk through" any dark valley, that is, to continue on our journey to the *more* of wholeness and holiness.

> Something,
> We know not what,
> Is always and everywhere
> Lovingly at work,
> We know not how,
> To make the world more than it is now
> To make us more than we are yet:
> One sacred heart, never apart.

4. *Loving as self-care.* We show respect for our bodies and our minds. Some of the saints engaged in ascetic practices that brought bodily harm to themselves. They believed that health-hazarding and life-negating practices were a source of merit or a way of joining in the sufferings of Christ. This is not our style now. We show respect for our body-minds. We take our cue from St. Francis, who engaged in over-the-top asceticism but on his deathbed repudiated that health-negating style. He said he regretted that he "was too hard on Brother Ass." Our style is do all it takes to become healthy in mind and body. They are the instruments of our calling, and we are committed to keeping them in good working order. We will never purposely harm ourselves. If we fast, we will do so within reason. It will not be a form of anorexia. Chastity will be motivated by bodily celebration, not fear of sex or denial of our need for it.

5. *Loving as responding to individual concerns.* We engage in the works of mercy toward individuals in our own community. We do this directly or by volunteering in or donating to a group that responds to their needs: "I was hungry and you gave me food, I was thirsty and you gave me something to drink, I was a stranger and you welcomed me, I was naked and you gave me clothing, I was sick and you took care of me, I was in prison and you visited me" (Matt 25:35–36).

We are grateful to be giving Jesus yet another opportunity to become incarnate as healer, this time right here, right now. We follow Jesus's commandment to love one another as he loved—and loves—us. We show our love to those around us, to those we meet. We feel and act with compassion toward all people. We do not hate anyone. We pray for those who have hurt us. We engage in daily acts of loving-kindness. We want those who offend us or others to see the light and be converted to a life of goodness rather than be punished.

6. *Loving as responding to social concerns.* Social issues abound: war, genocide, hate crimes, gun violence, discrimination, economic injustice, nuclear arms–building, ecological exploitation, climate change, torture, human trafficking, and homelessness. We can't focus on all of

them fully. The one that touches us the most is the one we are called to. Our being moved *is* how Christ is calling us. We are then animated with a passion to respond to the social cause that has become important to us. We transcend our comfort level, put ourselves out there for something we believe in. We speak up, become whistle-blowers. This may include heroic sacrifice. We act in accord with our God-given gifts and limitations. But no matter the style, we are doing the *most* we can do. Our heart has become the heart of Jesus and it is pierced, as his is, by human suffering. The piercing is the opening that lets through the light of compassion.

7. *Living the fruits of the spirit.* St. Paul lists the capacities for sanctity that can arise in us from the Holy Spirit: "The fruit of the Spirit is love, joy, peace, patience, kindness, generosity, faithfulness" (Gal 5:22). Our call to sanctity is to turn these gifts, by divine grace, into active virtues. We are grateful that they reside in us, and we focus on them, especially one each day, to bring them forward into our daily behavior: We practice *love* of God and charity to our neighbor. We feel *joyous* about our saintly yearnings and maintain an enduring optimism. We are patient, showing *forbearance*, especially with our own and others' inadequacies. We are *kind*, generous in giving others more than we believe we owe them. We show our *goodness* by coming across with an abundance of positive feeling for others. We are more concerned with being good than being right. We have *faith* in a divine plan and in an evolving humanity. We are faithful to others, never betraying their trust. We always choose the path of *gentleness*, no matter how others treat us. We do not allow abuse, and if it happens, we respond in nonviolent ways. We have *self-control*—set boundaries on our inflated ego—that seeks immediate gratification of its needs and wishes. We monitor our cravings and choose moderation. All this we do because we want to act in accord with the saintly capacities inside us. They are pathways to full discipleship: "My Father is glorified by this, that you bear much fruit and become my disciples" (John 15:8).

8. *Thanking.* Our yes to God's will—what is and what can be when love is the law of life—flows from and leads to gratitude. Dag Hammarskjöld's perfect prayer summarizes this quality of sanctity: "For all that has been, thanks. For all that shall be, yes." We are thankful for graces; we are thankful for opportunities to be vehicles of grace to others. St. Clare's last words show her sense of gratitude, even for being born: "Go safely and in peace, my so blessed soul. He who created you and sanctified you has always loved you tenderly, as a mother loves her little child. . . . And blessed be you, Lord, for creating me."[24] Gratitude is appreciation for what we are and have. It arises from deep within us where we find the gift dimension of all experience. Saints don't just say "Thanks," they become thanks. This leads to optimism about life as abundant, no scarcity inside or out. Gratitude for what we have also leads to compassion for those who lack what they need. A saint takes inequality as an invitation to be generous, and sees that apostolate not as an act of charity but as a choice for justice.

9. *Having a sense of humor.* In his book *Saints Are Not Sad,* Frank Sheed quotes St. Francis de Sales, who said, "A sad saint would be a sorry saint."[25] Theologian Edward Schillebeeckx adds, "Being sad in Jesus' presence [was] an existential impossibility."[26] Joy and its expression, humor, are central to sanctity.

In his *Poetics,* Aristotle noted that what is central to humor is not being disgusted by what is generally considered ugly. Saints see past ugliness and wickedness too, since compassion informs their sense of humor. Saintly playfulness is cheerful optimism about any predicament. It is never sarcasm or ridicule; it is always presented positively and in good fun. Connecting humor to psychological well-being is easy. Humor helps us adapt to fear, to be more at ease in anxiety-producing

---

[24] Quoted from the plaque over St. Clare's tomb in Assisi.

[25] Frank J. Sheed, *Saints Are Not Sad* (San Francisco: Ignatius Press, 2012), 5.

[26] Edward Schillebeeckx, *Jesus: An Experiment in Christology,* trans. Hubert Hoskins (New York: Crossroad, 1979), 201.

situations, to see more than one opportunity in a dilemma. Saints bring this mirthful energy into any experience to find an optimistic perspective. Humor is also a way of easing up on ourselves and others. It offsets the tragic with the innovative. We see another side, the *more*, more than what our one-track minds might make of a disaster. Saints are not happy all the time, but they are in touch with a joy that is deeper than any passing mood. From that gladness comes hopeful humor, a divine quality. Indeed, speaking about love of the things of this world, St. Augustine exclaims that the "world is a smiling place" (Sermon 158.7).[27]

10. *Sharing our good news with others.* We are sharing the joy of what we have found in the life of holiness, what we firmly believe in, and what inspires us. We act in accord with the twelfth step in the Alcoholics Anonymous program that speaks of having "a spiritual awakening" and carrying the message to others. Saint Madeleine Sophie Barat stated this beautifully in a letter to her sister religious of the Sacred Heart: "It is not merely for our own sakes that we should try to become interior souls; we should have constantly before our eyes the children who will come to claim spiritual help from us, help that without prayer we shall never be able to give them." We notice also in this quotation the importance of a prayer life in all our outreach.

St. Thomas Aquinas, reflecting Aristotle, wrote, "Goodness can't help but spread itself around." When we find an herb that works, we excitedly tell others so that they can try it. An able craftsman wants to pass his skill on to his child or apprentice. "Find" and "share" go together. Our instinctive generosity fosters the virtue of charity. The word "radiance" means *both* light and the emitting of light. We saints have a radiant calling.

> *At the center of the Universe is a loving heart that*
> *continues to beat and that wants the best for every*

---

[27] See also Peter Brown, *Religion and Society in the Age of St. Augustine* (Eugene, OR: Wipf and Stock, 2007), 32.

person. Anything that we can do to help foster the intellect and spirit and emotional growth of our fellow human beings, that is our job. Those of us who have this particular vision must continue against all odds. Life is for service.[28]

—FRED ROGERS (MISTER ROGERS)

---

[28]Acceptance speech when *Mr. Rogers' Neighborhood* won the 2001 Special Christopher Award.

26

Holy Affirmations

As a practice, we can use affirmations or prayers to place our ordinary behaviors into a sacred space—for example, "As I pet my dog, I offer affection to all creatures"; "As I peel this garlic, I remain aware of those who hunger and hope they find food in abundance. I make a contribution to a stop-hunger organization to help that happen." Values become virtues as we move from aspirations to plans.

> Graces keep coming my way and take me further
>   than my mind or will ever can.
> Grace meets me in every person.
> Grace finds me in every challenge.
> Grace carries me through every obstacle.
> I welcome the graces that come my way continu-
>   ally from people and circumstances.
> I am full of grace; something is working gracefully
>   in me.
> More and more, I am becoming a vehicle of grace.
> I am an emissary of light.
> I bring the light of consciousness to everything I
>   do and am.
> I keep tuning in to an abiding wholeness and holi-
>   ness within me.
> I release wholeness and holiness into the world.
> I treat this planet as a sacred thing.

I trust that everything is holy.

I release inner healing powers.

I am a source of miracles.

I carry the Grail of wholeness to every barren land in my life.

I live in constant contact with death-defying wholeness.

I am an epiphany of wholeness.

I am love, unconditionally flourishing in my human condition.

I am in the right place and time to love in saintly ways.

I show unconditional and universal love.

I feel a call to put myself on the line and engage in self-sacrifice to fulfill my destiny.

My destiny is to co-create a world of justice, peace, and love.

I am a hero of holiness.

I am humbled by my calling and my destiny.

I feel a call to be a saint.

I feel support from the communion of saints.

I feel held by divine feminine powers.

I am here to co-create, co-redeem, and co-sanctify the world.

I am here to give Christ another opportunity to live on earth for yet another lifetime.

I hear the voice of the Holy Spirit summoning me to live out the Sermon on the Mount.

I am thankful for all that has been and open to all that will be.

Now I see it all with compassion and holy amusement.

I trust I have all the graces I need to be sane, spiritual, and saintly.

Epilogue

Practicing Sane Love, Spiritual Love, Saintly Love

Love is a caring connection that is shown by giving and receiving the five A's outlined earlier in this book: attention, affection, appreciation, acceptance, and allowing. We may limit our love imagination and believe we can only show the five A's to those who are near and dear. We may not imagine the luminous joy of showing them boundlessly, far and wide, even to ourselves. In this book we have explored how far-reaching love is a reliable capacity in all of us, one of the graces of being human. Each one of us holds the full range of love's infinite extent, the full capacity to show love's richest graces.

The Buddhist practice of loving-kindness can help us practice the five A's limitlessly in psychological, spiritual, and saintly ways. It stretches our love to its wondrously abundant extent. Using this standard practice as a foundation, let's redesign it to integrate all three aspects: sane love, spiritual love, and saintly love.

The practice consists of declaring, feeling, and showing a caring connection in five concentric circles. The center circle is ourselves. The circle around ourselves comprises those with whom we are close, such as partner, relatives, and friends. The next circle includes those toward whom we are neutral, such as neighbors, acquaintances, and people we see and wave to or smile at in the course of our day but with whom we have no personal relationship. Next is the circle of people with whom we have conflicts—people we don't like, even enemies. Finally, there is the outer circumference, which includes all beings everywhere, those we will never meet or know.

In this practice we expand our loving-kindness, our affection, our caring, our compassion, our sense of loving connection, beginning with ourselves and extending it to everyone. We do this in two ways: by verbal aspiration and concrete actions.

Sane Love

We begin with an aspiration for what will be best *psychologically* for ourselves and others. We say aloud or silently each day:

> May I be happy, secure, and well.

We then make the same wish for each of the four surrounding circles of people listed above:

> May those I love be happy, secure, and well.
> May those toward whom I am neutral be happy,
>   secure, and well.
> May those with whom I have difficulty be happy,
>   secure, and well.
> May all beings be happy, secure, and well.

We might also use this same model in saying, "May I show attention, affection, appreciation, acceptance, and allowing to myself, those close to me, those to whom I am neutral, those with whom I have difficulty, all beings."

Spiritual Love

Next we aspire to and wish *spiritual* good for ourselves and others. As before, we begin with ourselves:

> May I be spiritually aware and awake. May I show com-
> passion. May I be a light in the world around me.
> May those I love be spiritually aware and awake.
> May they show compassion everywhere. May
> they be a light in the world around them.
> May those toward whom I am neutral be spiritual-
> ly aware and awake. May they show compas-
> sion everywhere. May they be a light in the
> world around them.
> May those with whom I have difficulty be spiri-
> tually aware and awake. May they show
> compassion everywhere. May they be a light
> in the world around them.
> May all beings be spiritually aware and awake. May
> they show compassion everywhere. May they
> be a light in the world around them.

Saintly Love

Finally, we apply our practice to a desire for *saintliness* in ourselves
and others:

> May I lead a saintly life and show the heart of God
> in all that I am and do.
> May those I love lead a saintly life and show the
> heart of God in all that they do and in who
> they are.
> May those toward whom I am neutral lead a
> saintly life and show the heart of God in all
> that they do and in who they are.
> May those with whom I have difficulty lead a
> saintly life and show the heart of God in all
> that they do and in who they are.

> May all beings lead a saintly life and show the
> heart of God in all that they do and in who
> they are.

Our capacity to love is indeed big enough to go this far. To say God is within us is to say that divine immeasurable love is within us. In such love, we can indeed feel a caring connection to all beings equally. We don't show our love in equal amounts or in the same way. We love our children differently than the way we love our next-door neighbor. The caring connection is one; the expressions of the caring connection are manifold.

The final part of the practice of loving-kindness is to show our loving-kindness in concrete ways. There is a list of specific examples in chapter 13 on integrity and loving-kindness. These examples are ways to act with affectionate caring and compassion to more of our fellow humans. We still love our family in special ways, but now we can love others in similar ways.

We are opening up within a love that is richer in its quality, larger in its quantity. We will soon notice graces coming *to* us. For instance, we automatically gain *equanimity*; we take things as they come with resilience. We are not so easily triggered and upset. Furthermore, as we show love, we may notice love coming to us, perhaps from unlikely quarters. The practice of loving-kindness takes us in both directions. We give and we receive.

As we begin this practice, we might think that it is selfish to love ourselves. The practice of loving-kindness, however, shows us the legitimacy of healthy self-caring. We might judge ourselves as unworthy of love. We judge ourselves to have been too often mean, inadequate, or unkind. Through loving-kindness, a door opens: our judgment of ourselves is redirected toward compassion for ourselves. Such self-compassion in the face of our self-judgment lays down new neural pathways in our brain. We begin to like ourselves more, grow in self-esteem. Consequently, we appreciate self-love not only as valid but we experience it as a source of growth.

As we hold our experience with patient gentleness instead of self-blame or shame, we embrace our limitations rather than become hemmed in by them. We trust, at last, that nothing about us has to get in the way of loving ourselves or others. Love, or God, has been waiting to make a personal appearance in our lifetime. By our loving-kindness practice it comes to pass, or rather, stays.

> *You are as prone to love as the sun to shine. Love is the true means by which the world is enjoyed: our love for others and their love for us. . . . If we cannot be satisfied by love, we cannot be satisfied at all. Never was anything in this world loved too much . . . but only in too short a measure. . . . The All is wholly within us and even then seems wholly without us. . . . It is an object infinitely great and ravishing: as full of treasures as full of room, as full of joy as of capacity. To blind men it may seem dark, but it is all glorious within, infinite in light.*
>
> —Thomas Traherne,
> seventeenth-century Anglican mystic,
> *Centuries of Meditations*

About the Author

David Richo, Ph.D., is a psychotherapist, writer, and workshop leader. He shares his time between Santa Barbara and San Francisco, California. Dave combines psychological and spiritual perspectives in his work. His website is davericho.com.

Other Books by the Author

How to Be an Adult: A Handbook on Psychological and Spiritual Integration (Paulist Press, 1991)

When Love Meets Fear: How to Become Defense-less and Resource-full (Paulist, 1997)

Shadow Dance: Liberating the Power and Creativity of Your Dark Side (Shambhala, 1999)

How to Be an Adult in Relationships: The Five Keys to Mindful Loving (Shambhala, 2002)

The Five Things We Cannot Change and the Happiness We Find by Embracing Them (Shambhala, 2005)

The Power of Coincidence: How Life Shows Us What We Need to Know (Shambhala, 2007)

The Sacred Heart of the World: Restoring Mystical Devotion to Our Spiritual Life (Paulist Press, 2007)

When the Past Is Present: Healing the Emotional Wounds That Sabotage Our Relationships (Shambhala, 2008)

Wisdom's Way: Quotations for Contemplation (Human Development Books, 2008)

Being True to Life: Poetic Paths to Personal Growth (Shambhala, 2009)

Daring to Trust: Opening Ourselves to Real Love and Intimacy (Shambhala, 2010)

Coming Home to Who You Are: Discovering Your Natural Capacity for Love, Integrity, and Compassion (Shambhala, 2011)

How to Be an Adult in Faith and Spirituality (Paulist Press, 2011)

How to Be an Adult in Love: Letting Love in Safely and Showing It Recklessly (Shambhala, 2013)

The Power of Grace: Recognizing Unexpected Gifts on the Path (Shambhala, 2014)

When Catholic Means Cosmic: Opening to a Big-Hearted Faith (Paulist Press, 2015)

You Are Not What You Think: The Egoless Path to Self-Esteem and Generous Love (Shambhala, 2015)

When Mary Becomes Cosmic: A Jungian and Mystical Path to the Divine Feminine (Paulist Press, 2016)

The Five Longings: What We've Always Wanted and Already Have (Shambhala, 2017)

Everything Ablaze (Paulist Press, 2017)

Five True Things: A Little Guide to Embracing Life's Big Challenges (Shambhala, 2019)

Triggers: How We Can Stop Reacting and Start Healing (Shambhala, 2020)